D0759552

3 1215 00080 2840

Men as Caregivers to the Elderly

Men as Caregivers to the Elderly

Understanding and Aiding Unrecognized Family Support

BY
Lenard W. Kaye
Bryn Mawr College
AND
Jeffrey S. Applegate
Bryn Mawr College

Lexington Books

D.C. Heath and Company/Lexington, Massachusetts/Toronto

Library of Congress Cataloging-in-Publication Data

Kaye, Lenard W.
  Men as caregivers to the elderly : understanding and aiding unrecognized
family support / by Lenard W. Kaye and Jeffrey S. Applegate.
    p.   cm.
  Includes bibliographical references and index.
  ISBN 0-669-19772-6 (alk. paper)
  1. Aged—Care—United States.   2. Caregivers—United States—Psychology.
  3. Men—United States—Psychology.   I. Applegate, Jeffrey S.   II. Title.
HV1461.K39 1990   90-6149
362.6—dc20   CIP

Published simultaneously in Canada
Printed in the United States of America
International Standard Book Number: 0-669-19772-6
Library of Congress Catalog Card Number: 90-6149

The paper used in this publication meets the minimum requirements of
American National Standard for Information Sciences—Permanence of
Paper for Printed Library Materials, ANSI Z39.48-1984. ∞ ™

Year and number of this printing:

90 91 92 8 7 6 5 4 3 2 1

To my wife, Susan I. Reisman
—L.W.K.

To Joan, Lauren, and Andy
—J.S.A.

Contents

Tables and Figures

Acknowledgments

T he authors acknowledge the assistance of numerous individuals who facilitated the research on which this book is based.

We are especially appreciative of the support received from the American Association of Retired Persons' Andrus Foundation, its Board of Trustees, Dr. Kenneth J. Cook, Administrator, and Mary Louise Luna, Research Associate. The study would not have been possible without AARP's financial generosity.

Margaret Zusky, Lyri Merrill, and Lee A. Young served as our editors at Lexington Books. Each was extremely helpful at different stages of publication.

A special note of thanks is due Geraldine McKenzie, the project's research assistant. Her contributions throughout all phases of this project, including a prominent role in the preparation of a practical guidebook for attracting men to caregiver support groups, are deeply valued.

Thanks are also due to Mirca Liberti and Louise Fradkin of Children of Aging Parents, Inc., for consulting with us from the outset and providing access to the CAPS national caregiver support group network.

Our expert panel, comprised of recognized scholars, administrators, and practitioners in the fields of gerontology, health care, and social welfare, were most generous in freely offering their time and expertise at several points during the course of this study. The panel included the following: Susan I. Reisman, Rohm and Haas Company; Dr. Gloria Heinemann, Buffalo Veterans Administration Medical Center; Dr. Cynthia Stuen and Dr.

Amy Horowitz, New York Association for the Blind (The Lighthouse); Dr. Estelle Greenberg, The Brookdale Foundation; Dr. Toba Kerson, Dr. Cynthia Brownstein, and Dr. Greta Zybon, Bryn Mawr Graduate School of Social Work and Social Research; Dr. Neal S. Bellos, Syracuse University; Dr. Margaret Donnelly, Lehman College, City University of New York; Jessica Getzel, Jewish Home and Hospital for the Aged; Dr. Mary Ann Lewis, Fordham University; Dr. Richard Machemer, St. John Fisher College; Joan Mintz, New Jersey Division on Aging; Fran Pratt, Center for Understanding Aging; Dr. Robert Rubinstein, Philadelphia Geriatric Center; Bernice Soffer, Coalition of Advocates for the Rights of the Infirm Elderly; Dr. Carol C. Riddick, University of Maryland; Barbara H. Rinehart, Lenox Hill Neighborhood Association; Meryl Drake, Supportive Older Women's Network; Dr. Robyn Stone, National Center for Health Services Research and Health Care Technology Assessment; Anna H. Zimmer, Hunter College; Mirca Liberti and Louise Fradkin, Children of Aging Parents, Inc.; Dr. Ann Burack Weiss, Columbia University; and Dr. Susan R. Sherman, State University of New York at Albany. We are also grateful to Madalyn Turnbull for her continued input and interest.

Members of the Bryn Mawr College community were instrumental in facilitating the administrative and budgetary execution of the research project, including Dean Ruth W. Mayden, Steven Bell, Nona Smith, Diane Craw, and Adrienne D'Amato. Carolyn Wilson, Renna Van Oot, Linda Kiefer, Hannah Kaufman, Janet White, Alexis Hillman, Amy Scheier, Nancy Ignatin, and Sister Mary Jude engaged in critical supportive activities including interviewing, coding, and data entry. Kate Kraft deserves special recognition for expertly carrying out all computer analytic tasks. Much appreciation is due as well to Lorraine Wright, Peg McConnell, and Elaine Robertson for their word-processing expertise and unfaltering patience throughout the course of project activities. Peg McConnell took lead responsibility for preparing the final book manuscript.

Finally, we extend our sincere thanks to all those male caregivers, elder care receivers, and support group leaders throughout the United States who gave their time to respond to our numerous research questions and inquiries. Their thoughtfulness and honesty were critical to the success of this investigation.

Of course, the authors assume full responsibility for the interpretations and conclusions contained in this book.

Introduction

Today the familiar characterization of the American family as "in transition" is an anachronism. Though the idea of the family endures, its structure and role allocation are in a process of transformation. Especially striking are changes in the ways families are caring for their dependents across the life cycle. Shifts in child care are most conspicuous. Many of the burgeoning number of mothers in the work force, for example, turn to day care and ask their male partners to share a greater proportion of the tasks of child rearing. Since the 1970s the dilemmas faced by two-career couples trying to maintain the fragile balance between working and parenting have attracted abundant scholarly and popular attention.

Less recognized but equally profound in their impact are shifts in the ways families are taking care of those whose dependency appears at the end of the life cycle. As they step onto the threshold of the twenty-first century, families feel a steady increase in the already substantial pressure to care for their infirm elderly relatives. In the wake of a period of diminishing formal supports for America's swelling ranks of aging citizens, the responsibility for their care lands squarely in the laps of their children, spouses, and other kin. And these caregivers, enjoying the prospect of increased life expectancy but having the lowest birth rate since World War II, ask the unsettling question, "Who will take care of me?"

Traditionally, the answer to this question has been spoken in the female voice. Study after study documents what most families know from experience: Women have taken care of the frail old people in their families, extending careers of caregiving that often included care of infants, children, and spouses. But the late twentieth-century "baby bust" means there will be fewer women to fulfill this role in the future; and, as more of them go to work outside their homes, the flexible free time they need to provide elder care diminishes. Moreover, today's women are less willing than those of previous generations to take on caregiving responsibilities automatically. Distressingly, many must try to do it all, ending up subject to a pernicious triple jeopardy as they try to find room in their lives to meet the conflicting demands of their growing or grown children, full-time employment, and elder caregiving.

The spotlight of research has illuminated the needs of this at-risk majority more and more clearly. As a result, what we know about elder caregiving applies primarily to female elder caregiving. Standing in the shadows just beyond the spotlight are the husbands, sons, sons-in-law, brothers, and other men who take care of their frail elderly. Though still a minority, they constitute up to a third of primary caregivers in some settings; and as families continue to change and conceptions of gender roles broaden, their numbers are likely to grow.

Who are these unsung heroes? What do they do, how do they feel about it, and how does it affect their lives? What is it like for them to be deeply engaged in what society has defined as "women's work"? And how well does the network of formal support services respond to their needs? The goal of this book is to answer these and other questions about the male caregiver for the elderly and, in doing so, to help move him out of the shadows.

The answers presented here emerge from a national and local study supported by a generous grant from the Andrus Foundation of the American Association of Retired Persons. At the national level, a sample of men caring for an elderly relative, leaders and organizers of caregiver support groups, and a panel of experts in elder caregiving responded to survey questionnaires designed to yield an expanded body of information about the special experiences and needs of caregiving men. In personal interviews, a smaller sample of male caregivers and the elderly recipients of their care living in greater metropolitan Philadelphia shared their perceptions of the unique frustrations and rewards of their caregiving arrangements. The resulting range of data sources yields both a broad description of the male elder caregiving experience and a more subjective, intimate portrait of individual men whose day-to-day lives take shape around the care of another—often a woman.

Our strategy for presenting the results of this study is an integrative one. Although the national and local samples differ in composition, their demographic characteristics are remarkably similar. Therefore, rather than present data from the samples separately, we have chosen to amplify data from the national group with illustrative vignettes reported by local caregivers and elder recipients. The outcome of this strategy is a method of reporting the findings that moves back and forth between broadly drawn composite sketches of the male elder caregiver and individual close-ups that capture intersubjective dimensions of his task. The hope is that, by offering this combination of perspectives, the book will lend direction to gender-sensitive service delivery, program planning, policy formation, and future research.

The Plan of the Book

Chapter 1 reviews the current status of family elder caregiving in the United States, focusing specifically on sociodemographic trends that increase the likelihood that more men will move into the primary caregiving role. Chapter 2 looks at some of the ways in which traditional sex role socialization has defined elder caregiving as women's work, thus presenting men who become caregivers with unique challenges and dilemmas. Our research methods are described in chapter 3; and chapter 4 presents profile data on the study's male caregivers and the recipients of their care.

In chapter 5, we present findings related to the patterns of assistance our respondents received from both formal and informal sources of support. In chapter 6, we examine the frequency, competence, and satisfaction with which the men performed a wide variety of caregiving tasks as well as some of the barriers that impeded their task performance. Chapters 7 and 8 report results related to the men's caregiving relationships and attitudes. And we look at their use of and experience in caregiver support groups in chapter 9. In chapter 10, we present some implications of the study findings for service delivery and suggest directions for future research. In the appendixes that conclude the book we provide details of scale and index construction, a set of practical recommendations for engaging men in caregiver support groups, and a basic glossary of statistical terms used in the text.

1

Family Elder Caregiving in the United States: An Old Song in a New Key

The vast majority of families take care of their frail elderly relatives. They always have, and the likelihood is that they always will. A spate of studies documents that families—not formal service personnel—predominate as providers of health care and other services to the burgeoning ranks of America's impaired elderly (Cantor 1983; McAuley & Arling 1984; Shanas 1979; Stoller 1983; Stone, Cafferata & Sangl 1987). This arrangement has survived changes in family composition, industrialization, modernization, bureaucratization, and the increased geographic mobility of families (Paillat 1976; Sussman & Cogswell 1972). Popular rhetoric that today's Americans have abandoned their elderly to the impersonal care of nursing homes finds no support from research. To the contrary, 95 percent of old people and 90 percent of those who are physically impaired live at home where spouses, children, or other relatives provide the bulk of their care ("Mothers bearing" 1989).

Although the tradition of family elder care endures, the character of the family providing this care has changed dramatically. A remarkable convergence of demographic, political, and ideological trends is virtually transforming the family, reconfiguring its topography, and pulling it in new and often conflicting directions. Bolstered by health care advances and declining mortality, the family is expanding vertically. More and more families can boast three, four—even five—generations (Lowy 1986). While the U.S. population as a whole has tripled since the beginning of the century, the proportion of those 65 years old and older has increased eightfold (Shanas 1984). By 2030 the entire baby boom generation—77 million people—will be senior citizens (Beck 1989). Largest increments will occur in America's oldest old, those 85 and older for whom some form of chronic illness, disability, and, thus, dependency is a virtual certainty. Given present trends, by 2080 there will be three million people between the ages of 95 and 99 years old and more than a million over 100 (U.S. Bureau of the Census 1989).

Counterbalancing this unprecedented vertical expansion in families is a horizontal shrinkage. A steadily declining birthrate, expected to continue dropping through the 1990s, will leave potential elder caregivers in short supply (Sherman, Ward & LaGory 1988). The resulting demographic chasm between growing elder need and diminishing family resources portends a disturbing scenario for the twenty-first century: A vast army of people whose advanced age and frailty assures that they will need to depend on others for basic care, and a relatively small cohort of close relatives to provide this care.

The spectre of this disparity is particularly sobering in light of the reality that the United States is already nearing its absorptive capacity to provide formal supports to elderly citizens and their family caregivers. This impending saturation point is in part a legacy of the New Federalism, a set of Reagan-era policies that reduced or eliminated scores of federally sponsored programs available to families. This dwindling of formal services reinforces politically the traditional societal admonition that families should "take care of their own"—including, of course, their own infirm elderly (Sussman 1985).

Taking care of the elderly is not, however, what it used to be. Lingering chronic illnesses have replaced the acute diseases that accounted for most deaths early in the century (Brody 1986). Old people with these conditions require the most physically demanding and emotionally taxing kinds of caregiving; and predictions are that more than 70 percent of them will require assistance with routine activities of daily living (Longino 1988).

Rather than accommodating this shift in health status, however, current public policies and programs seem to ignore or oppose it, trapping many caregiving families in a perilous Catch 22. While elders' health problems call for long-term care, most health care policies and programs cover only short-term care (Moore 1983). Medicare, the largest government payor of health care for the elderly, focuses almost exclusively on acute hospital care. And Medicare's prospective payment system, enacted in 1983, works to shorten hospital stays by reimbursing hospitals a preset amount for each patient's care according to Diagnostic Related Groups (Fischer & Eustis 1988). This system, though perhaps fiscally efficient, returns the sick elderly to their families "quicker and sicker," often in need of high levels of supportive care (Kaye 1988). But federal programs do little to help caregivers maintain elders at home. In 1986, less than two percent of Medicaid and Medicare budgets went to home care (Hooyman & Lustbader 1986). Many families try to fill the resulting service gaps by piecing together and orchestrating a complex network of informal and formal supports. Beyond their roles as concerned helping relatives, these caregivers find themselves learning to be expert case managers (Seltzer, Ivry & Litchfield 1987).

States have tried to take up some of the slack in formal services, many offering some form of payment to relatives who provide home elder care (Linsk, Keigher & Osterbusch 1988). Other programs such as tax credits or deductions and respite care are also helpful, although most fall far short of compensating for the losses in time and money sustained by caregiving families.

Even where formal services are available, many families appear curiously reluctant to use them. Results from a recent study of family caregivers suggest that they have internalized an expectation that they should try to avoid outside assistance as long as possible (Noelker & Bass 1989). Forty-two percent of those surveyed used no formal services. Apparently many caregivers "spend down" their emotional as well as their financial resources before seeking help.

This attitude derives in part from Americans' longstanding commitment to self-sufficiency, a value currently finding reaffirmation in a "new familism" that endorses the centrality of the

family as the primary caregiving group (Hartman 1981). Embedded in this ideology is a fierce independence that places high
value on "going it alone" and "doing it myself," regardless of
the costs.

Family Caregiving: The Costs are Great

The costs of family caregiving are usually high. In addition to
financial expenditures, caregivers pay a price in decreased physical and emotional well-being, diminished participation in work
and social activities, and increased tension in marital and family
relationships. When compared with noncaregivers in a recent
study, caregivers averaged three times as many stress symptoms,
took more psychotropic drugs, and reported substantially less
participation in social and recreational activities. Those living
with the care recipient were at greater risk for stress symptoms
and decreased life satisfaction. Spousal caregivers appeared especially vulnerable, exhibiting lower levels of well-being and reporting significantly lower incomes than caregivers who were
adult children or other relatives (George & Gwyther 1986). In
another study, 70 percent of caregivers reported health problems
associated with the strains of their responsibilities (Snyder &
Keefe 1985).

Though intuitively it seems that caregiving for an institutionalized relative would be easier than home care, this is not always
the case. Though different, it may not be less stressful. One
study found that, overall, levels of burden experienced by those
persons looking after someone in a nursing home did not differ
from those caring for an elder in the community (Pratt, Wright
& Schmall, 1987).

Regardless of the caregiving setting, one of the factors making the task so stressful is that it is added on to, and frequently
competes with, the other day-to-day obligations of busy families
(Bowers 1987). Recent figures indicate, for example, that between 30 and 55 percent of elder caregivers work outside the
home (Opinion Research Corporation 1989; Scharlach & Boyd
1989). Most are neither in a financial position nor motivated to

give up their jobs. But almost three-quarters find that caregiving interferes with their work lives in ways that range from making them late ("Caregiving's toll" 1989) to increased absenteeism and missed career opportunities (Scharlach & Boyd 1989).

Whatever the pragmatics of caregiving arrangements, there is voluminous evidence that the subjective dimensions override all others in predicting the impact of taking care of an elderly relative on someone's life (Gwyther & George 1986). It is the interpersonal and intrapsychic factors that take the highest toll. Caregiver well-being appears to be related to the nature of the relationship and other contextual factors more than to the severity of the impaired elder's health status and related needs for hands-on care (George & Gwyther 1986; Zarit 1982; Zarit, Reever & Bach–Peterson 1980). In a recent study by Sheehan and Nuttall (1988), those caregivers reporting most interpersonal conflict with the recipients of their care also reported most strain. In contrast, those reporting high levels of reciprocal affection with recipients experienced less stress and depression—a finding replicated in research by Stoller and Pugliesi (1989). Especially for spouse caregivers, however, the intense dependency involved in caregiving may produce a troublesome paradox: the dependency that forges closer emotional ties between caregivers and recipients may also render day-to-day interactions less enjoyable (Horowitz & Shindelman 1983). Feelings of guilt, anger, remorse, and sadness may intrude in the closest of relationships in uncharacteristic and often uncomfortable ways.

The Benefits of Caregiving

The obvious burdens and liabilities of elder caregiving tend to obscure its gratifications and rewards—dimensions of the experience that have received little attention from researchers (Motenko 1989). Yet among the motivations for caregiving are love, affection, reciprocity, commitment, and a sense of pride (Graham 1983; Horowitz 1985a; Johnson 1985; Motenko 1988). Family elder caregiving occurs in a context of emotional attachment and intimacy, permitting caregivers to express new levels of closeness in their relationship.

Again, intersubjective factors dominate in determining the meaning of caregiving. In one study, for example, those providing care out of reciprocity and nurturance experienced more gratification from their tasks than did those who gave care out of a sense of duty. Relationship variables overrode both the duration of caregiving and the severity of the recipient's symptoms in influencing the degree of gratification (Motenko 1989). Another group experienced primarily a sense of pride in caring for their disabled spouses (Motenko 1988). For some caregivers, nurturing a loved one provides an opportunity for anticipatory grieving that may help them deal with the eventual loss of the recipient (Vinick 1984).

Taking care of a frail elderly relative is a complex undertaking influenced by a range of objective and subjective factors. Caregiving should be neither catastrophized nor idealized; it can be both draining and richly rewarding. It turns the life cycle upside down, transforming parents into children and children into parents. For spouses, it transports the marital relationship into new territories of dependency and intimacy for which socialization offers few maps. Whatever its meaning to individual families, caregiving alters their relationships with their elder loved ones in ways that close some doors and open others.

Women and Caregiving

So far we have spoken about caregiving in gender-neutral language. But in the language of the real world of elder care, the term family caregiver usually translates to *female* family caregiver. Study after study documents that an unpaid female relative, usually a daughter or daughter-in-law, steps into the primary caregiving role when an elderly person in the family needs help (Brody 1981, 1985, 1986; Horowitz 1985a, 1985b; Montgomery & Kamo 1987; Sherman, Ward & LaGory 1988; Snyder & Keefe 1985; Stone, Cafferata & Sangl 1987). In most research samples, between two-thirds and three-quarters of elder caregivers are women, and they spend an average of 16 hours a week in this role (Wood 1987). They live closer to and have more frequent contact with their families of origin than do men (Troll, Miller & Atchley 1979); and they provide more hands-on personal care for elderly relatives than do male caregivers, who are more likely to help with less intimate tasks such as home repair and maintenance and financial management. (Rathbone–McCuan & Coward 1985; Young & Kahana 1989).

Traditional Western sex-role socialization has prepared women to assume nurturing roles for their families across the life cycle. But more influential is the pragmatic reality that women's roles as homemakers have permitted them more flexible free time for elder caregiving than men have had (Horowitz 1985b). The exploitation of this availability has promoted a feminization of caregiving that makes it a women's issue in the truest, political sense of the term (Sommers 1985).

But this flexible availability among women is disappearing as families change to meet the demands of contemporary American life. The previously cited trend toward smaller families means that there are and will continue to be fewer female offspring to provide elder care. And both financial imperatives and career goals dictate that more women work outside the home. Those who do have less to give to caregiving (Stueve & O'Donnell 1989). Currently, at least half of all working-age women are employed. Among those aged 45 to 54—the cohort of "women in the middle" (Brody 1981) most likely to be entangled in a web of competing demands from growing or grown children, a husband, and a needy elder relative—64 percent are in the work force (Schick 1986). Apparently they are not cutting down on work time to be caregivers, but rather are trying to add on to it. In one sample, being employed reduced the average level of a son's caregiving assistance by 20 hours a month; but a job did not reduce the level of daughters' assistance significantly (Stoller 1983). Clearly these women, trying to do it all, are likely candidates for role overload and probable burnout. Their plight underscores the crucial necessity of studying and promoting alternatives to traditional patterns of family elder caregiving for the 1990s and beyond.

The Turn toward Men

Given the trends described above, it is likely that men will be called on increasingly to absorb some of the responsibility for elder caregiving. Recent research suggests that, although daughters and daughters-in-law continue to shoulder the bulk of the load of caring for aging parents, many sons are moving into this role (Brody 1986; Horowitz 1985b; Montgomery & Kamo 1987; Rathbone–McCuan & Coward 1985; Snyder & Keefe 1985; Stoller 1983). And when the focus shifts to spousal caregivers, the caregiving gender gap narrows (Pruchno & Resch 1989). A growing literature documents that more husbands are becoming primary caregivers for their ailing wives (Davies, Priddy & Tinklenberg 1986; Fitting & Rabins 1985; Hlavaty 1986; Motenko 1988; Vinick 1984; Zarit, Todd & Zarit 1986). Because more women than men are diagnosed with Alzheimer's disease, the crushing caregiving burdens associated with this disease are especially likely to fall to husbands (Fitting, Rabins, Lucas & Eastham 1986).

Part of the shift toward male elder caregiving can be attributed to what Shanas and her associates (1968) refer to as the principle of substitution: men step in to help an aging relative when wives, adult daughters, daughters-in-law, and other female relatives can no longer do so. But this scenario fails to account for the husbands, sons, grandsons, brothers, and other men who have been primary elder caregivers from the beginning, and whose lives are dominated by their caregiving roles. These men, many of them deeply embedded in what they have been socialized to view as women's work, have been "unsung and understudied" (Barrow 1986). They are pioneers in uncharted territory, whose approach to caregiving, interacting with increasingly flexible conceptions of gender roles, may render them uniquely adapted to meet the elder caregiving challenge of the twenty-first century.

2
Gender Patterns in Elder Caregiving

The gender role polarization between the female world of caregiving and the male world of economic providing is rooted in traditional sex role socialization of children. Men who become elder caregivers, therefore, take on a role that is likely to challenge long-held conceptions of who they are and what they should be doing. Although both men and women have the inherent potential to nurture and care for others, they receive early messages from parents, teachers, and others that send them in different directions.

Bakan (1966) proposes two fundamental modalities—agency and communion—that are characteristic of all life forms. Agency concerns the individual organism as a separate entity and manifests itself in self-protection, self-assertion, and self-expansion. Communion concerns the organism in relation to the larger body of other organisms and expresses itself in a sense of connection with others. Bakan asserts that the viability of organisms depends on their capacity to balance and successfully integrate these two modalities so that neither dominates the other.

Earliest psychological development, however, seems to impede rather than support this integration. The need to establish a core gender identity leads boys and girls down divergent intrapsychic and interpersonal paths. Whereas girls can establish a female self-definition while retaining a primary identification with their mothers, boys must forcefully separate from and disidentify with their mothers in order to identify with their fathers and consolidate their maleness. As a result girls tend to forge a personal identity based on attachment while boys define themselves through separation (Cath 1983; Chodorow 1978). Masculinity becomes associated with agency, femininity with communion.

Western sex role socialization further promotes this gender-role bifurcation. From birth, parents treat girls in ways that foster connectedness with others while encouraging separation and distancing in their boys. They provide girls with toys that promote imitation and are likely to be played with in proximity to the mother. Boys, in contrast, receive toys that encourage creative manipulation, provide explicit feedback from the outside world, and are used away from the mother. Boys are permitted more freedom to explore and engage in unsupervised activities than are girls, who are told to stay close to home. Similarly, parents assign girls homebound chores like cleaning, helping mother, and babysitting, whereas boys' chores, such as mowing the lawn or taking out the garbage, send them out of the house. Both primary and secondary school teachers reinforce this differential socialization in the classroom (Block 1984).

These findings, building on those of Parsons and Bales (1955) and Barry, Bacon, and Child (1957), underscore what we know from experience: Masculinity becomes associated in this culture with an instrumental, agentic, cognitive emphasis on "getting the job done," while femininity evolves into an expressive, communal, and affective concern with the well-being of others. Men come to know the world in terms of separation, while women's ways of knowing have more to do with interpersonal connection (Belenky, Clinchy, Goldberger & Tarule 1986). In terms of moral development, women's grounding in connectedness cultivates in them an ethic of caring and responsibility that orients them toward empathic relationships with others. Men, in contrast, are schooled in an ethic of justice that focuses on the rights and rules of relationships (Gilligan 1982).

In this culture, these gender distinctions take on a political cast. Since the industrial revolution, when men left rural families to go to work in the cities, women's work of mothering, homemaking, and kinkeeping has been accorded secondary economic status, while men's work of providing has received an elevated status (Livson 1983). Accordingly, caregiving, whether it be childrearing or elder care, has been assigned to women and viewed as less prestigious than work outside the home. Traditionally, then, women have engaged in careers of caregiving at the domestic center of the family while men have kept their distance at its perimeter (Gutmann 1987).

Gender and Elder Caregiving

How do these dimensions of sex-role socialization influence the male elder caregiver? For one thing, a man who assumes primary caregiving confronts challenges to his earliest and most fundamental self-conceptions. Brought up to be agentic, instrumental, and to emphasize cognitive over affective aspects of experience, he meets in caregiving a series of tasks that require his close emotional involvement. Socialized to provide and protect, he is now asked to nurture, to undertake what he has come to think of as women's work.

Predictably, quantitative research comparing male to female caregivers appears to confirm stereotypic conceptions of gender role allocation. A traditional division of labor is particularly true of sons and daughters caring for their parents. Rathbone–McCuan and Coward (1985) found that daughters were eight times more involved in household chores and three times more likely to give personal care to their parents than sons. Sons, in turn, were nine times more likely than daughters to provide home repair and maintenance. Similarly, Horowitz (1985b) learned that, with the exception of health care, daughters were more likely than sons to give hands-on personal assistance to their parents. In more gender-neutral or traditionally male-oriented tasks such as financial management, financial assistance, or dealing with bureaucratic organizations, sons' involvement did not differ significantly from that of daughters. And sons had a more limited time and task commitment to caregiving than did daughters—a finding echoing that of Montgomery and Kamo (1978). Along the caregiving continuum, as a dependent parent's need for assistance progresses from a need for help with business matters and transportation to a need for more personal care, women are more likely to move into a primary role.

This primary caregiving role exacts a high price. Female caregivers tend to take more psychotropic drugs, report more symptoms of stress, and participate in fewer recreational and social activities than do male caregivers (George 1984). They also report lower morale (Gilhooly 1984) and higher levels of burden than do their male counterparts (Barusch & Spaid 1989; Young & Kahana 1989). In one study of spousal caregivers, women seemed to have difficulty detaching emotionally from the responsibilities of care, while men approached their tasks in a more instrumental, task-oriented manner (Zarit 1982). Interestingly, in a two-year follow-up of this sample, this difference in coping styles was no longer apparent (Zarit et al. 1986). The researchers suggest that, over time, wives may have assumed the more instrumental, task-focused approach originally observed for husbands.

Overall, female caregivers do appear to struggle more than men with balancing their caregiving responsibilities with obligations to others and self (Pratt, Schmall & Wright 1987; Young & Kahana 1989). Men's "getting-the-job-done" approach may help them keep greater emotional distance from their caregiving tasks, and thus may shield them from some of the guilt, depression, and feelings of burden suffered by female caregivers. Or, as Davies, Priddy, and Tinklenberg (1986) suggest, men may learn to mask their feelings more effectively, living out the prevailing stereotype that they should "bear up" and suppress evidence of personal vulnerability.

This defense appears to have operated for 25 widowers who recalled the experience of caring for their disabled wives (Vinick 1984). They reported that their tasks ranged from housework to feeding, toileting, bathing, grooming, and other aspects of personal care; and only one complained of having to do "women's work." Though they described personal experience with restricted mobility, social isolation, and chronic lack of sleep, they did so in a typically stoic, matter-of-fact way that betrayed few feelings about these inconveniences. Their minimization of hardships made it difficult to know how to plan services for them.

Indeed, several other studies suggest that, in contrast to women, men tend not to use caregiver support groups (Hlavaty 1986; Snyder & Keefe 1985). Those who do attend welcome information and appear more concerned with the concrete issues of care provision than with discussing their feelings (Davies, Priddy & Tinklenberg 1986).

Given traditional sex role socialization, this coping style is what we would expect from male elder caregivers. But some recent qualitative studies render a more complex picture that challenges the stereotypes. Looking more closely at issues of context and meaning, these ethnographic case studies capture nuances of caregivers' subjective experience that larger studies often overlook. Six older men caring for their impaired wives, for example, appeared to be performing labors of love and commitment, which they enjoyed and in which they took pride (Motenko 1988). Motivated both by their appreciation for the care and support their wives had provided them earlier and by a desire to keep a meaningful relationship alive, these men derived heightened self-esteem and feelings of security from caregiving. Moreover, their identities appeared to be "embedded entirely in their caregiving activities" (Motenko 1988, 113).

These men did not appear to be masking hidden feelings; they were quite open in reporting considerable stress. But this stress was associated with feelings of loss rather than with caregiving burden. They wanted neither relief from caregiving nor did they want someone else to take over. Rather than lengthy periods of respite, they preferred ongoing support that would permit them to continue their primary tasks. They wanted responsibility for and control over the caregiving situation.

Miller (1987) suggests that this interest in being in charge is an extension of men's traditional role of authority both at work and at home. Men in her sample of those caring for cognitively impaired spouses appeared to experience less stress if they were more in control of the caregiving situation. Similarly, the Quayhagens (1988) found a puzzling negative correlation between respite time and well-being for husbands taking care of a wife with Alzheimer's disease, suggesting that men felt better if they were around to oversee the situation.

Although this emphasis on control may be tied in part to the social reinforcement men receive for taking charge, ethnographies like Motenko's (1988) demonstrate that men also derive gratification from opportunities to nurture. While their wishes to pay back their wives for the care bestowed on them earlier may be based on an ethic of justice, their caregiving also appears to express an ethic of caring and connectedness (Gilligan 1982).

Male Caregiving and the Move toward Androgyny

Many male caregivers arrive at the caregiving role at a point in the life cycle when they are naturally becoming more expressive and nurturant. Husbands are especially likely to become caregivers to their wives at late mid-life or old age—a time when research suggests that they move toward a more feminine self-definition (Lewis & Roberts 1982; Neugarten 1968). In contrast to the rigidly polarized sex roles to which they are likely to have been oversocialized earlier in their lives, post-parental men tend to describe themselves in more complex, androgynous terms (Sinnott 1984). They retreat from the perimeter of the affective life of the family toward its domestic center, a process that Gutmann (1987) terms the "feminization" of older men. This process enables men to reclaim and enjoy the full range of masculine and feminine self-dimensions, to recapture the sexual bimodality that they suppressed earlier in order to fulfill society's expectations that they concentrate on economic providing for young families. Levinson and his associates (1978) suggest that this integration of masculine and feminine polarities is the principal task of adult development in men. Resulting androgyny is associated with enhanced self-esteem, increased role flexibility, and other indicators of psychological health and well-being (Bem 1974; Boles & Tatro 1982). Elder caregiving, therefore, may offer men the chance to free up previously unexpressed strivings and, in doing so, to expand the boundaries of the self.

This shift assumes special importance in light of findings suggesting that mid-life women naturally become more agentic, independent, and instrumental in their self-definitions. Previously socialized to immerse themselves in caring for others while suppressing autonomous strivings, post-parental women become more assertive, achieving, and self-sufficient (Gutmann 1987; Livson 1983; Lowenthal, Thurnher and Chiriboga 1975; Neugarten 1968).

The intersection of these life-cycle developmental shifts in both sexes with elderly relatives' needs for caregiving means that providing elder care may be dissynchronous for women but synchronous for men (Pruchno & Resch 1989). Perhaps the high stress levels in female elder caregivers occur in part because this responsibility opposes their natural developmental direction. And male caregivers may experience less stress because they have found a role that is congruent with their mid- and later-life developmental priorities.

The Influence of the Women's Movement

Reinforcing these life-cycle shifts are social changes that support increased participation by men in elder caregiving. Gains realized from the women's movement permit women more freedom to exercise their agentic, instrumental strivings earlier in the life cycle and to find alternatives to careers of caregiving that begin with childrearing and end with taking care of their parents, in-laws, or spouses (Kaye & Applegate 1990). By the same token, late twentieth-century men have more permission from society to express their proclivities for nurturance and tenderness. Results of this loosening of rigid sex roles for men are most apparent in patterns of parenting. Fathers of infants and young children appear increasingly skilled and comfortable at being "maternal" (Applegate 1987; Cath, Gurwitt & Ross 1982; Pedersen 1980; Pruett 1987). These new nurturant fathers often forfeit a competitive edge in the workplace in order to make time for child care. And many report new levels of personal growth and fulfillment as a result.

Perhaps these nontraditional men will move into elder caregiving roles more comfortably than have their predecessors. Since projections are that more and more men will be called upon to take care of their elders (Horowitz 1985b; Fitting & Rabins 1985), this would be a desirable outcome. As men assist, augment, or replace the elder caregiving efforts of women, it is crucial to understand the unique vulnerabilities and strengths they are likely to bring to this role.

3
Study Methodology

The Study Purpose and Questions

This study was conducted with the purpose of developing a much-needed reservoir of information about the special experiences and needs of male caregivers and their elderly relatives. To this end, a three-tiered research project was carried out during the period January–December 1988, which incorporated: (1) a national survey and analysis of men engaged in the elder caregiving experience; (2) an intensive local assessment of male caregiver and family care receiver experiences in Pennsylvania and New Jersey's Delaware Valley area; and (3) the performance of brief program development surveys with a recognized panel of gerontological, health, and social welfare experts.

The following questions formed the conceptual infrastructure for the study:

1. What are the attitudes, expectations, and needs of men acting as caregivers to their elderly relatives?

2. What are the distinctive characteristics and coping strategies of men performing this role?

3. What are the factors that instigate the allocation of elder caregiving to men in families?

4. What are the incentives and disincentives for successful male caregiving performance?

5. What are the unique interpersonal relationship dynamics that influence the quality of caregiving interchanges between males and their dependent relatives?

6. To what extent have family caregiver support groups responded to the unique needs of male caregivers?

Answers to these questions were intended to give direction to the development of a series of practical guidelines that could assist both professionals and lay organizers in designing programs that will effectively engage and support men in family caregiving.

Preliminary Activity

Prior to the construction of the research questionnaires, a series of meetings were held with selected members of the expert panel, including executive staff of Children of Aging Parents, Inc., a national networking organization dedicated to helping develop caregiver support groups in communities throughout the United States. These sessions helped identify the key issues that influence the caregiving experience and support group participation. An updated review of the literature, including analysis of current research reports on various aspects of elder caregiving, was also useful in pinpointing pivotal variables to be subjected to further analysis. These reports were utilized as well to identify a range of scales, indices, and related measures that could be adopted in original or modified form for this research. In particular, we sought to identify those protocols that did not reflect a gender bias.

The national survey collected data from support group leaders associated with a national sample of freestanding and affiliative caregiver support groups. These groups were drawn from two sources: (1) the National Council on Aging's 1985 *Idea Book on Caregiver Support Groups*, which includes a national directory of 266 caregiver support groups in 38 states and the District of Columbia (NCOA 1985); and (2) the 1987–1988 national roster of 125 family caregiver support groups for which Children of Aging Parents, Inc., (CAPS) has provided educational programs and resources, information and referral, and individual peer counseling. The combined initial total for the two national support group listings was 371. When corrected for support group duplications, disbanded or discontinued groups, etc., the number was reduced to 233.

In order to look more intensively at some of the parameters of male caregiving examined in the national survey of caregivers and leaders, a series of extended interviews was conducted with male elder caregivers in the Greater Delaware Valley (Southeastern Pennsylvania and Southern New Jersey) and, where possible, with the recipients of their care. The majority were members of support groups affiliated with Children of Aging Parents, Inc. The plan was to interview 30 caregiver–recipient pairs. Although the pairs were easily identified through the local caregiver support group network, it soon became clear that the majority of men were providing care for recipients too impaired to be interviewed. As a result, although all 30 male caregivers were interviewed, only 9 of the 32 persons they were caring for (two men were each caring for two relatives) could be similarly questioned. Most of those unable to be interviewed had dementia that was secondary to Alzheimer's disease. Two were in nursing homes and had dementia. Two were deaf and/or unable to speak.

Efforts to identify additional subject pairs in which the recipient could be interviewed failed. A major finding from this part of the study, therefore, was that most of the local male caregivers were caring for recipients who were profoundly impaired. In one poignant example, a male caregiver said that, although his mother could be interviewed, she might seem "a little confused at times." When the interviewer met her and began to interview, it became clear that she was totally disoriented and believed that her parents, long dead, were providing her care. It appeared that her son was able to sustain his caregiving role only by employing considerable denial of the extent of her dementia and other disabilities.

Finally, a national panel of 26 gerontological experts in family caregiving, long-term care, and aging was identified and contacted at two different points during the course of the project. Experts represented colleges and universities, gerontology institutes and centers, medical centers, community service programs, private foundations, and government agencies.

Eventually, 152 support group leaders and 148 male participants in caregiver support groups completed structured survey
questionnaires. These represent response rates of 65 percent for
group leaders and 65 percent for male group members. The
group leader response rate is based on a maximum allowable
return of one questionnaire per caregiver support group. The
male caregiver response rate is based on a maximum allowable
return of one questionnaire for each caregiver support group
reporting a single male participant and two questionnaires for
each caregiver support group reporting two or more current participants who are male. (Group leaders were asked to distribute
up to two male caregiver questionnaires to those males who had
been members for the longest period of time.)

The Survey Instruments

Structured survey instruments were constructed for the two major groupings of national respondents: (1) support group leaders,
and (2) male participants in support groups. Semistructured
questionnaires were designed for the face-to-face, local interviews
with male caregivers and elder care recipients. Expert panel
members were administered a structured "variable identification"
questionnaire earlier on in the study and a semistructured "program development" questionnaire later into the investigation.
The nature of each instrument is briefly discussed below.

A. The Male Caregiver Support Group
Member Questionnaire

This instrument aimed to gather a series of baseline data along
several dimensions of caregiving. Issues of concern included:

1. The range and type of caregiving functions performed;

2. The incentives and disincentives to family caregiving by
   men;

3. The recipients of male caregiving;

4. The quality of male caregiver/care recipient relationships;

5. The techniques employed by males in carrying out the caregiving function; and

6. The extent to which self-help, mutual aid, and professional caregiver support programs have been responsive to the special needs of the male caregiver.

The male caregiver support group member questionnaire consisted of 74 questions and required 45 minutes to 1 hour to complete. Both descriptive and attitudinal or normative responses were solicited. A mix of open-ended and closed-ended or forced-choice questions was included. In addition to a series of original questions constructed especially for this research, a number of previously developed measures and indices were utilized in rendering operational the study variables. In some cases these indices were modified to serve better the purposes of this research. Only those measures considered to be gender neutral or bias free in terms of the gender of the caregiver were selected for use. Table A–1 in appendix A summarizes the specific measures developed by other authors that were used in this instrument.

B. The Caregiver Support Group Leader and Organizer Questionnaire

This instrument was designed to gather data similar to that collected by means of the male caregiver questionnaire. However, in this case, leaders of groups were asked to respond to questions based on perceptions of the dominant experiences of those men who participated in their particular caregiver support group. In addition, this questionnaire sought data reflective of the structure, function, operating procedures, and experience of conducting a caregiver support group. The questionnaire was structured (included open- and closed-ended probes), contained 65 questions, and required 30–45 minutes to complete.

C. The Greater Delaware Valley Male Caregiver Field Interview

This instrument was designed to facilitate intensive face-to-face interviews with male caregivers. A semistructured field question-

naire was designed that allowed caregivers to respond in a personal manner to the same set of research questions considered at
the national level, including the incentives and disincentives associated with caregiving, the nature of the caregiver–care recipient
relationship, and the extent to which caregiver support groups
and similar programs reflect adequate sensitivity to the needs of
the male caregiver. A larger proportion of questions in this questionnaire was open ended than in the national survey questionnaires. A total of 69 questions comprised this instrument, and it
required approximately 1 hour to complete.

D. The Greater Delaware Valley Elder Care Recipient Field Interview

This field guide was comprised of 16 open-ended probes allow-
ing elder care recipients maximum flexibility in responding to
interviewer questions. Questions addressing satisfaction levels,
the skills of the caregiver, comparisons between male and female
caregiving ability, and recipient preferences concerning caregiving
were included. A total of 16 general probes were included re-
quiring 20–30 minutes to complete by the interviewer.

E. The Expert Panel Assessment Instruments

The expert panel completed two survey questionnaires during the
study. The first questionnaire (covering four issue areas) asked
members to assess the degree of importance a series of factors
play in understanding particular dimensions of male caregiving.
The dimensions addressed included: (*a*) the disincentives or barriers to male caregiving involvement; (*b*) the factors influencing
the intensity (quality and quantity) of male caregiving involvement; (*c*) the incentives for male caregiving; and (*d*) the influences on the psychological and emotional status of the male
caregiver–dependent elder interpersonal relationship. This questionnaire helped us identify key factors or variables for further
analysis in the study.

The second expert panel survey instrument was a nine-
question assessment sheet comprised of open-ended probes addressing the methods, techniques, and strategies for successfully

engaging men in caregiver support groups. Expert panel members provided recommendations as to: outreach and recruitment strategies; improvements in the structure and frequency of meetings; style of group leadership; location of meetings; and type of sponsorship or auspice of support groups. Appropriate group content, needed skills and attributes of group leaders or organizers, and special training needs were also addressed.

Data Collection

The first wave of national survey questionnaires was mailed in March 1988 to the two directory lists of caregiver support groups. Designated caregiver support group leaders and organizers received instruments. They also received two male caregiver instruments for distribution to those male participants of longest standing in the group. Cover letters advised all potential respondents of the study's intent, the voluntary nature of the survey, and the fact that the names of all participants would remain confidential. Initial followup letters were mailed to leaders and organizers in May 1988, with second requests mailed in June 1988.

During June through August 1988 telephone interviews were conducted with all nonresponding leaders. This procedure resulted in the further identification of disbanded or inactive support groups, as well as a marginal increment in the number of leaders willing to respond to the survey.

Interviews with male caregivers and elder care recipients in Pennsylvania's Greater Delaware Valley commenced in April and continued through October 1988. Prior to this phase of the research, field interviewers participated in three separate days (six hours) of orientation and training in interviewing technique. Coder training was offered as well. Interviews with caregivers and care recipients were conducted in the respondents' homes during separate sessions. All face-to-face interviews began with the reading of a brief explanation of the nature and intent of the study and a request from the interviewer that the interviewee sign the "Statement of Explanation Form." Assurances of confidentiality and anonymity were given at this time as well as a review of the voluntary nature of the study. It is worth repeating that the severely deteriorated physical and mental status of many of the elder care recipients precluded the conduct of interviews with a significant number of them. In other cases, only small portions of the questionnaire could be completed. In several cases, elder care recipients had recently died or been institutionalized.

The initial mail survey of the expert panel (Time 1) was administered in November and December 1987. The subsequent survey (Time 2) of program development recommendations was carried out in August and September 1988.

Data Analysis

The National Sample

All completed questionnaire responses were numerically coded and then entered into data files using SPSSX, a statistical software package for research in the social sciences. Resultant data files were subsequently subjected to computer analysis. Descriptive statistics (frequencies and percentages) were computed as well as higher order statistics including Pearson correlations, t tests, and one-way analysis of variance. Reliability coefficients were computed where necessary. Factor analytic procedures were carried out for selected sets of study variables. Brief explanations of these procedures and other statistics used in this project can be found in appendix C.

A major vehicle for data analysis was the application of a series of existing and original indices tapping a range of dimensions of caregiving. Ten indices were adapted from earlier studies by Bem (1974), Center for the Study of Aging and Human Development (CSAHD) (1978), Heller (1970), Horowitz and Dobrof (1980), Hudson (1982), Irelan, Rabin, and Schwab (1987), Shanas (1962), Smilkstein (1978), and Zarit, Reever, and Bach–Peterson (1980). These indices measured Family Function, Quality of Relationship, Illness, Activities of Daily Living, Behavioral

Orientation, Financial Health, Life Satisfaction, Sex Role, Familism, and Burden. Prior to statistical analysis, selected index items were recoded in order to insure consistency in terms of the direction of response choice valuation. The aforementioned measures were found to have moderate to high levels of internal reliability or consistency for this study (as determined by means of the coefficient alpha statistic—see appendix C for further explanation).

Eight additional indices created for the current study (Task Frequency, Task Satisfaction, Task Competence, Barriers to Caregiving, Recipient Affection, Provider Affection, Service Receipt, and Service Need) were similarly found to be internally reliable (at moderate to high levels of measurement) and were therefore employed in the analysis. Table A–2 in appendix A identifies the number of index items and internal consistency measures for each composite measure employed. Once again, individual item response choices were recoded where necessary to make consistent the direction of their valuation prior to statistical analysis. The soundness of these indices and individual items is argued on both face validity and construct validity grounds. The indices' face validity is argued on the grounds that other professionals in the field have used the individual index items in the past to define the variables in question. Furthermore, the original survey of the expert panel (at Time 1) served to separate out those items believed to play a particularly significant role in understanding the contributions of various dimensions of male caregiving. These items were subsequently incorporated in selected composite study measures. As will be documented in later chapters, the fact that certain indices are able to produce different scores for respondent subgroups believed to have different opinions or experiences related to the measure strengthens the argument for construct validity.

Items in three study indices—Task Frequency, Barriers to Caregiving (male caregiver), and Sex Role—were factor analyzed in order to identify more detailed dimensions of the study constructs based on potential groupings that distinguished sets of items from each other. Those factors that displayed eigenvalues greater than 1.0 and contained three or more items were consid-

ered (see appendix C for further explanation). Those factor loadings (the correlation between each item or variable and the
factor) that related to the pattern at 0.45 and above were chosen
to define the factor. In those few instances where an item loaded
at 0.45 or above on more than one extracted factor, the higher
of the two loadings became the criterion for dimensional repre-
sentation. Thus each index dimension was comprised of a mutu-
ally exclusive set of items.

Once identified, each set of index factors was standardized
by using average item scores in all analyses. The factors identified for the Task Frequency Index were subsequently employed
in the analyses of the Task Competence and Task Satisfaction
Indices. (These three indices contained identical sets of index
items). Similarly, the factors extracted from the Barriers to Caregiving Index administered to male caregivers were employed in
subsequent analyses of the Barriers to Caregiving Index administered to support group leaders and organizers. Again, in this
case, the items contained in the two indices were identical. This
technique allowed for comparative assessments of male caregiver
experience across three aspects of task performance and across
the two respondent data bases in the case of caregiving barriers.
Table A–3 summarizes information about the factored dimensions for the six indices including the factor reliabilities.

Appendix A also includes definitions of each of the study
indices and factors and includes related statistics.

The Local Sample

Data gathered during interviews with the small sample of caregivers and recipients from the Greater Delaware Valley were
analyzed by hand. Simple frequency tabulations produced descriptive statistics; we performed a content analysis on the narrative responses elicited by open-ended questions in the interview
protocols. Wherever possible, categories into which these narrative data were organized paralleled the categories employed to
organize quantitative data from the national sample.

Because the local sample was demographically similar to the
national sample, we chose to report data gathered from each

group in combined form. In other words, rather than report qualitative findings gathered from Greater Delaware Valley respondents in a separate section, we used them to amplify or illuminate quantative findings from the national sample. The result is that reports of statistics from the national sample are interspersed with illustrative quotations from local respondents.

4
Who Are the Partners in Care?

In this chapter, descriptive data characterizing the three central participants in the caregiving process are presented and discussed. Male caregivers, elder care recipients, and support group leaders constitute the caring partnership. As we see it, each of these groups of individuals influences the caregiving experience in unique ways. Husbands, sons and, other men in the family constellation deliver the actual care. The elder spouse, mother, or father receives this much-needed aid but is also responsible for shaping the quality of the caregiving experience and the relationship that evolves between provider and recipient. The support group leader is strategic in ensuring that the caregiving experience remains sound and endures over time.

These data are intended to establish a framework from which a greater understanding of the male caregiving experience can be developed.

Characteristics of Male Caregivers

The age of the respondents at the time of the survey ranged from 36 to 84 years. As shown in table 4–1, the majority of the male caregivers were age 60 or older, with a mean age of 68 years. Twelve caregivers were age 80 or older. Seven in 10 male caregivers were married and living with their spouses. Twenty-nine were married and living apart from their spouses. Only 5 percent of the respondents were divorced, separated, or widowed. Six never married.

It should be noted that the overwhelming majority of the respondents in this research were white. Those remaining were

Table 4–1
*Age, Marital Status, Race, Ethnic Origin, and Religion
of Male Caregivers*

		Number	*Percentage*
Age			
Under 40		3	2.0
40–49		9	6.1
50–59		15	10.2
60–69		45	30.5
70–79		64	43.1
80–89		12	8.1
Mean = 68	Total	148	100.0
Marital status			
Never married		6	4.1
Married, living with spouse		106	71.6
Married, living apart from spouse		29	19.6
Divorced/separated		4	2.7
Widowed		3	2.0
	Total	148	100.0
Race			
Asian		1	.7
Black		4	2.8
White		138	95.8
American Indian		1	.7
	Total	144	100.0
Ethnic origin			
German		43	33.1
Italian		4	3.1
Irish		12	9.2
French		6	4.6
Polish		3	2.3
Russian		2	1.5
English		28	21.5
Scottish		4	3.1
Welsh		3	2.3
Afro-American		4	3.1
Other		21	16.2
	Total	130	100.0
Religion			
Protestant		92	64.3
Catholic		28	19.6
Jewish		9	6.3
Other		14	9.8
	Total	143	100.0

Asian, black, or American Indian. The ethnic origin of the caregivers was primarily German, English, and Irish. Sixty-four percent were Protestant, 20 percent were Catholic, and 6 percent were Jewish.

The majority of the male caregivers were retired (see table 4–2). Of those caregivers who were in the workforce at the time of the survey, 43 percent identified themselves as professionals, administrators, or managers. Approximately the same percentage of retired caregivers reported being in this professional category.

The vast majority of the respondents had a high school education, and thirty-nine percent had a college education or beyond. The household incomes of the caregivers ranged from under $10,000 to more than $50,000. Forty-four percent earned between $20,000 and $50,000 per year, while 8 percent earned less than $10,000.

Interestingly, the data indicate that the men in our survey assumed caregiving responsibilities despite the presence of other potential caregivers. More than four-fifths of the respondents had living children. Over three-fourths had living grandchildren. Fifty-one percent of the men had living brothers and 62 percent had living sisters.

The sample was dominated by male caregivers who owned their own homes and lived with others. Eighty-two percent of the respondents lived with at least one family member, while 5 percent lived with one or more nonrelatives. It should be noted that more than three-fifths of the male caregivers resided with the person to whom they provided care. Interestingly, nearly 83 percent of the caregivers who lived with the care recipient had lived with them for more than 20 years.

The Local Male Caregivers

The demographic characteristics of the 30 male caregivers from the Greater Delaware Valley were strikingly similar to those of the national sample. There was a six-and-a-half year average age difference: the mean age for the national was 68 years whereas that for the local sample was 61 years. This discrepancy, however, appears to be more a statistical artifact than a substantive

Table 4–2

Employment Status, Educational Background, and Household Income of Male Caregivers

		Number	Percentage
Employment status			
Employed, full time		28	19.5
Employed, part time		10	6.9
Retired		104	72.2
Other		2	1.4
	Total	144	100.0
Occupation of employed caregivers			
Professional		10	26.3
Manager/administrator		8	21.1
Sales work		10	26.3
Clerical/office work		4	10.5
Service work		4	10.5
Other		2	5.3
	Total	38	100.0
Usual occupation of retired caregivers			
Professional		27	26.0
Manager/administrator		18	17.3
Sales work		8	7.7
Clerical/office Work		3	2.9
Service work		12	11.5
Other		36	34.6
	Total	104	100.0
Education			
Grammar or grade school		5	3.5
Some high school		12	8.4
High school		39	27.2
Some college		29	20.3
College		28	19.6
Some graduate school		12	8.4
Graduate school		15	10.5
Other		3	2.1
	Total	143	100.0
Household income			
0–$9,999		11	7.9
$10,000–$19,999		45	32.1
$20,000–$29,999		26	18.6
$30,000–$39,999		21	15.0
$40,000–$49,999		14	10.0
More than $50,000		23	16.4
	Total	140	100.0

difference. The existence of two very young (27- and 28-year-old) caregivers pulled the mean of the small local sample down. The overall age distributions, however, were parallel. Other differences included a slight variation in religious affiliation—there were more Catholics in the local sample—and a larger proportion of "never married" men in the local group.

Characteristics of Elder Care Recipients

Table 4–3 shows that more than 90 percent of the persons being cared for by the male caregivers in the study were female. Sixty-three percent of the care recipients were between the ages of 60 and 79 years; 29 percent were aged 80 or older. Only 7 percent of the care recipients were under age 60.

The majority of the care recipients were married and living with their spouses (62 percent). Like the males in our study, nearly all were white and had English, German, or Irish heritages. More than half of the care recipients were Protestant.

The data showed that the majority of the elders being cared for by the male caregivers were well educated (see table 4–4). Nearly 75 percent had a high-school education or beyond. Slightly more than one-quarter of the care recipients had careers as professionals, managers, or administrators. Ten percent had worked in service positions.

Interestingly, more than half of the care recipients lived in a private home which they owned. Approximately one-fourth lived in a nursing home. It should be noted that more than one-third of the care recipients lived with their husbands, 12 percent lived with their children, and 8 percent lived alone.

The Local Care Recipients

As was the case with the male caregivers, the demographics of the small sample of elder care recipients from the Greater Delaware Valley closely resembled those of the national sample. The sole exception was that a larger proportion of the national sample were married and living with a spouse.

Table 4—3
Sex, Age, Marital Status, Race, Ethnic Origin, and Religion of Care Recipients

		Number	Percentage
Sex			
Male		12	8.2
Female		134	91.8
	Total	146	100.0
Age			
Under 60		11	7.5
60–69		34	23.2
70–79		59	40.0
80–89		35	23.9
90–99		8	5.4
	Total	147	100.0
Marital status			
Never married		6	4.1
Married, living with spouse		92	62.2
Married, living apart from spouse		24	16.2
Divorced/separated		1	.7
Widowed		22	14.8
Other		3	2.0
	Total	148	100.0
Race			
Asian		2	1.4
Black		4	2.7
White		142	95.9
	Total	148	100.0
Ethnic origin			
German		27	19.9
Italian		4	2.9
Irish		19	14.0
French		4	2.9
Polish		2	1.5
Russian		3	2.2
English		2	1.5
Scottish		2	1.5
Welsh		5	3.7
Afro-American		4	2.9
Other		15	11.0
Don't know		7	5.1
	Total	136	100.0
Religion			
Protestant		97	66.0
Catholic		31	21.1
Jewish		5	3.4
Other		14	9.5
	Total	147	100.0

Table 4–4

Occupation, Education, Background, and Living Arrangements of Care Recipients

		Number	*Percentage*
Occupation			
Professional		32	22.2
Manager/administrator		7	4.9
Sales work		4	2.8
Clerical/office work		27	18.8
Service work		15	10.3
Other		59	41.0
	Total	146	100.0
Education			
Grammar/grade school		16	10.9
Some high school		18	12.2
High school		47	32.0
Some college		27	18.4
College		18	12.2
Some graduate school		7	4.8
Graduate school		9	6.1
Other		5	3.4
	Total	147	100.0
Housing			
Private house, rent		2	1.4
Private house, own		87	59.2
Apartment		8	5.4
Townhouse		5	3.4
Boarding home		1	.7
Life care center, retirement		1	.7
Nursing home		35	23.8
Other		8	5.4
	Total	147	100.0
Household composition			
Lives alone		11	7.7
Lives with wife		13	9.1
Lives with children		17	11.9
Lives with grandchildren		3	2.0
Lives with mother		1	.7
Lives with father		0	0
Lives with brother(s)		1	.7
Lives with sister(s)		2	1.4
Lives with other relative(s)		10	7.0
Lives with friend(s)		5	3.5
Lives with boarder(s)		3	2.1
Lives with nonrelative/paid help		7	4.9
Lives with husband		53	37.1
Lives with other		17	11.9
	Total	143	100.0

Characteristics of Group Leaders and Organizers and Their Male Group Members

As shown in table 4–5, the majority of the support group leaders who responded to our surveys were between the ages of 30

Table 4–5

Age, Sex, Educational Background, and Employment Status of Support Group Leaders

		Number	Percentage
Age			
Under 29 years		10	7.0
30–39 years		35	24.5
40–49 years		46	32.1
50–59 years		27	18.9
60–69 years		15	10.5
70–79 years		7	4.9
80 years and older		3	2.1
	Total	143	100.0
Sex			
Male		16	10.9
Female		131	89.1
	Total	147	100.0
Education			
Grammar or grade school		0	0
Some high school		1	.7
High school		6	4.1
Some college		12	8.3
College		26	17.9
Some graduate school		22	15.2
Graduate school		78	53.8
	Total	145	100.0
Employed?			
Yes		128	87.1
No		19	12.9
	Total	147	100.0
Occupation			
Professional		102	80.3
Manager or administrator		15	11.9
Sales work		1	.8
Clerical or office work		4	3.1
Other		5	3.9
	Total	127	100.0

and 49. Fewer than 1 in 5 were 60 years of age or older. The sample was dominated by female support group leaders.

The vast majority of the group leaders had a minimum of a college education. More than half completed graduate studies. Nearly all of the group leaders were employed, mostly in professional positions.

The data indicated that slightly more than half of the support group leaders were elder caregivers at some time in their lives. Surprisingly, more than 40 percent were not. Of those leaders who had caregiving experience, most had cared for their mothers, fathers, or spouses.

The sample was dominated by leaders who held their positions for extended periods of time. More than 60 percent of the respondents had served as leaders for more than two years.

Slightly more than half had received specialized training before assuming the role of support group leader. Of those leaders who had been trained, most had received thirty or more hours of formal preparation. The most common types of training were professional preparation in social work, counseling, or a related field.

There was great variation in the ways that group members were seen as perceiving the leaders' role. Approximately equal proportions perceived the leader to be an expert, moderator, or friend. A smaller number saw the group leader as representing a fellow caregiver or a therapist.

As shown in table 4–6, the support group leaders reported that more than 60 percent of their male group members were 60 years old or older. Less than 8 percent were younger than age 40. In contrast to these data, the men responding to our survey, as reported in table 4–1, tended to be older.

Support group leaders also reported a slightly more diversified racial composition than did the male caregivers. Whites, however, continued to dominate.

According to the group leaders, approximately one-third of the male group members were employed full time, and 1 in 10 were employed part time. Fifty-seven percent of the men worked in white-collar jobs, and the vast majority of leaders felt the men in their groups were managing "fairly well" or "very well" financially.

Table 4–6
Support Group Leaders' Characterization of Male Group Members

	Number	Percentage
Age of cohorts		
Under 30 years	5	1.8
30–39 years	16	5.6
40–49 years	30	10.5
50–59 years	56	19.6
60–69 years	75	26.3
70–79 years	68	23.9
80–89 years	33	11.6
90 years and older	2	.7
Total	285	100.0
Race		
Asian	5	4.1
Black	10	8.2
Hispanic	2	1.6
White	104	85.3
American Indian	1	.8
Total	122	100.0
Employment status		
Full time	59	31.4
Part time	22	11.7
Retired	100	53.1
Unemployed	5	2.7
Other	2	1.1
Total	188	100.0
Type of work		
White collar	88	56.8
Blue collar	67	43.2
Total	155	100.0
Financial well-being		
Very good	40	32.3
Fairly good	80	64.5
Not good	4	3.2
Total	124	100.0
Number who live with care recipient		
0	48	32.4
1–3	57	38.4
4–6	35	23.6
7–9	4	2.8
10 or more	4	2.8
Total	148	100.0

Caregiver Financial Health

The financial health of the male caregivers was measured by combining the responses to two questions from the Social Security Administration's Retirement History Survey (Irelan, Rabin, and Schwab 1987). The questions were designed to gauge the caregivers' self-assessments of their state of financial satisfaction and security. Responses reflected relatively high levels of self-perceived financial health among respondents. Mean scores on the individual items and the composite index were situated between "very well" and "fairly well."

There were no significant differences in self-perceived financial health when marital status, employment, cohabitation with care recipient, and presence of Alzheimer's disease were considered. Similarly, the age of the caregiver and the length of time he attended a caregiver support group were not significantly associated with financial health.

On the other hand, the level of formal education and physical health of the caregiver did correlate significantly with financial well-being. As expected, the financial health of caregivers increased with advanced levels of education. Better physical health was also positively associated with heightened financial health.

Physical, Functional, and Emotional Health

This section presents data on the physical, mental, and functional health status of the study's male caregivers and their elder care recipients. Four health indices were used to measure the severity of recipient illness, recipient capacity to perform activities of daily living, the extent of recipient behavioral dysfunction, and caregiver life satisfaction. These data serve to make more precise and multidimensional the profile of caregivers and care recipients developed in the preceding section.

Health Problems of the Care Recipient

When caregivers were asked to specify which of twenty-one health problems their impaired elders suffered from, the most frequently reported physical ailments were arthritis or rheumatism, poor sight, and poor hearing. These items comprised an index that is a slightly modified version of a composite measure of health problems developed earlier by Shanas (1962). A complete description of this measure appears in appendix A. The mean summary score on the Illness Index was actually quite low, only registering 0.15 on a two-point scale on which 0 = "absence of disease" and 1 = "presence of disease".

As shown in table 4–7, age and educational level as well as the caregivers' characterization of the impaired elders' overall health registered statistically significant correlations with the Illness Index ($p < 0.05$ or greater). Specifically, older, lesser-educated elders with lower levels of caregiver-characterized overall health suffered from more health problems. On the other hand, statistically significant correlations were not evident between the Illness Index and the length of time the caregiver had cared for the impaired elder or the caregivers' characterization of the impaired elders' mental or emotional health.

Though the association between the care recipients' age and the Illness Index was relatively weak, it nevertheless confirms the expected—that physical health deteriorates with advancing age. It is more difficult to explain a weak but statistically significant relationship between the care recipients' educational attainment and the Illness Index. Caregivers with more advanced education had fewer physical ailments. Finally, a moderately strong correlation existed between the Illness Index and the caregivers' characterization of the impaired elders' overall health. As one would expect, a low overall health rating was associated with an increased number of physical ailments.

Activities of Daily Living and the Impaired Elder

Male caregivers were assisting persons who required significant amounts of time and attention on a daily basis. The Activities of Daily Living (ADL) Index, developed by Horowitz and Dobrof

(1980) and described in detail in appendix A, measures the degree of impairment associated with the care recipients' performance of daily living activities. The Index contains fifteen items and is scored on a three-point index where 0 = "no difficulty," 1 = "some difficulty," and 2 = "must have help." Care recipients were assessed as experiencing significant difficulty in performing activities of daily living. The mean score on the ADL Index was situated midway between "some difficulty" and "must have help," confirming substantial functional incapacity among recipients. The most difficult activities for impaired elders to perform included handling money, shopping for groceries and other things, getting to places outside of walking distance, and preparing meals. Clearly, care recipients were perceived as being unable to care adequately for themselves without assistance from a caretaker. A notable association was found between the ADL Index and the mental health status of the caregiver. The findings indicated that as recipients' ADL limitations increased, caregivers reported a lower rating of their own mental health status. The relationship between these two variables is worrisome, suggesting that caregivers may be increasingly vulnerable to the strain of caregiving at the very time when their services are needed most.

Significant correlations were found between the ADL Index and the following three variables: the length of time the caregiver had provided care for the impaired elder, the caregivers' characterization of the impaired elders' physical health, and the caregivers' characterization of the impaired elders' mental health (see table 4–7). All three associations were moderately strong and were statistically significant. These findings indicate that restrictions in the impaired elders' performance of daily living activities increase with the length of time the caregiver has provided assistance and with the deterioration of the elders' mental and physical health. Decline for the care recipient is cumulative and widespread, extending across the functional, physical, and emotional domains.

Care Recipients' Mental or Emotional Health Status

When asked to assess the impaired elders' mental or emotional health status, the male caregivers gave ratings of "fair" to

Table 4–7

Pearson's Correlations for Illness Index, Activities of Daily Living
Index, Behavioral Orientation Index and Selected Study Variables

Study variable:	I	II	III	IV	V
Illness Index	.26**	.09	−.19*	−.43***	.12
Activities of Daily Living Index	−.12	.43***	−.04	−.39***	.35***
Behavioral Orientation Index	−.05	.10	−.07	−.05	.39***

  I = Age of care recipient
 II = Length of time caregiver has cared for impaired elder
III = Level of education of care recipient
 IV = Caregiver's characterization of impaired elder's overall health
  V = Caregiver's characterization of impaired elder's mental or emotional health
  *p < .05
 **p < .01
***p < .001

"poor." This finding is further supported by caregiver assessments of the impaired elders' degree of behavioral orientation. Behavioral "health" was measured by the nine-item Behavior Orientation Index. This composite measure of mental health is based on a series of interviewer assessment items found in the Older American Resources and Services (OARS) Multidimensional Functional Assessment Questionnaire (CSAHD 1978. A complete description of this measure is found in appendix A. The index aims to gauge the extent of inappropriate behavior displayed by the impaired elder. The mean summary score on the Behavioral Orientation Index indicated that caregivers observed "occasional" mental impairment or behavioral disturbance in the persons they cared for. Behaviorally inappropriate actions were most typically displayed in the form of mentally confused or disoriented behavior and fear or anxiety. Elders were least likely to be characterized as being excessively talkative or jovial and full of unrealistic physical complaints. In addition, it is striking to note that 81 percent of the male respondents in this study reported that they believed their care recipients suffered from Alzheimer's disease or a related disorder. In combination, these data make clear that the male caregivers participating in this research were caring for severely mentally incapacitated persons.

A relatively weak but significant association was found between the ADL Index and the Behavioral Orientation Index. It is interesting that such a relationship was not evident between the Illness Index and the ADL Index. This further emphasizes that male caregivers cared for persons who exhibited a combination of rather severe functional and mental frailties rather than severely disabling physical illnesses.

A separate analysis considered differences in caregiving experience in relation to the nature of the kinship between caregiver and care recipient. Significant differences were found between elders being cared for by a spouse and those receiving care from other relatives. Impaired elders who were married to their caregivers were found to have fewer health impairments than other care recipients. On the other hand, spousal care recipients appeared to experience greater difficulty performing daily living tasks than did nonspousal care recipients. Spousal care recipients were also judged to have significantly lower levels of mental or emotional health compared to nonspousal care recipients. Similarly, they were more likely than nonspousal care recipients to have Alzheimer's disease or a related disorder and to display behavioral disturbances or mental impairments. These findings are in line with others suggesting that male spouse caregivers frequently care for women who have significant cognitive and behavioral disturbances (Barusch & Spaid 1989). It would seem that the poor mental health of the spousal care recipient was intimately tied to her inability to perform daily living activities. However, poor physical health in nonspousal care recipients did not appear to impede their activities of daily living.

Overall Health Status of Male Caregivers

In general, male caregivers perceived themselves to be in relatively good health. This was supported by the group leaders' characterization of their male members' overall health. However, when asked if their health in any way limited the care that they provided to their impaired elders, more than 40 percent of the caregivers said that it did. This suggests that the physical demands of caregiving can be exceedingly burdensome, even for men who are reportedly in good health. As one gentleman in the local group of Greater Delaware Valley respondents put it, "When you're old, you get tired. If you were feeling good and wanted to do it, you'd be OK."

Male Caregivers' Mental or Emotional Health Status
and Life Satisfaction

Caregivers who were in poor physical health were likely to suffer difficulties in other areas of their lives. A relatively strong association existed between the caregivers' self-assessed overall health status and their mental health status. Caregivers who had lower levels of assessed overall health were likely to assess their mental health in more negative terms as well.

In general, it can be said that the data revealed only moderate-range assessments of the male caregivers' emotional or mental health. Both male caregivers and support group leaders indicated that the caregivers' mental health status was situated only at the midpoint of a 4-point "excellent" to "poor" scale. The responses to several additional questions pertaining to the caregivers' satisfaction with life supported this rating. Mean scores on these survey probes once again reflected only moderate levels of personal satisfaction among male caregivers in terms of feelings of loneliness, frequency of worrying, general perceptions of life, and overall satisfaction with life. Taken together, these measures comprised a Life Satisfaction Index, a composite measure drawn from the OARS Methodology (CSAHD 1978). Summary scores on the index confirmed that the male caregivers' personal contentment in life was rated as only "fair." One elderly man caring for his brain damaged wife spoke the sentiments of many: "[my life] could be worse; could be a whole lot better."

It is noteworthy that levels of caregiver satisfaction did not significantly vary across a range of respondent subgroups. Thus, life satisfaction levels did not alter with respect to caregiver employment status, caregiver age, caregiver financial health, caregiver marital status, or level of caregiver education. Similarly, caregiver life satisfaction levels were unchanged when considering whether or not frail elders had Alzheimer's disease, whether or not caregivers were married to care recipients, and whether or not they resided in the same household. Finally, life satisfaction levels were not correlated with caregiver self-rated mental or emotional health.

It would appear that the men engaged in elder caregiving in this research did not express significantly divergent views of their personal well-being. A series of health-related and socioeconomic profile variables was not particularly helpful in understanding under what conditions this sense of personal contentment might have wavered. Further analysis will be needed to discover what dimensions of elder caregiving may indeed play a role in understanding a male caregiver's changing view of the quality of his personal circumstances and his relative position in the caring partnership.

Summary

In summary, male caregivers were likely to be white, over sixty years old, married and living with their spouses. The majority were retired high-school graduates who perceived themselves as financially healthy. More than three-fifths of the caregivers lived with the person to whom they provided care.

Similarly, elder care recipients were predominately female, white, and over age sixty. Most lived with their spouse in a private home.

Support group leaders typically were female, between the ages of thirty and forty-nine, and college educated. Most had elder caregiving experience and had been involved with their support groups for an extended period of time. Approximately half received formal training before assuming their leadership role.

Male caregivers did not feel their impaired elders were extremely physically disabled or frail. Most frequently, physical health problems centered around the difficulties associated with arthritis and rheumatism or sensory impairment. Older, less educated elders suffered from more health problems.

Whereas assessments of care recipient physical health problems may have been minimized, functional capacity was not. Caregivers observed care recipients to have substantial difficulty in performing the basic activities of daily living. Functional incapacity increased during the course of caregiving, accompanied by declines in care recipient physical and mental health.

The mental health of care recipients was also judged to be substantially impaired (this was especially the case for the wives of male caregivers). The vast majority of men believed their relatives were suffering from Alzheimer's disease or a related disorder. Mentally confused or disoriented behavior combined with excessive expressions of fear and anxiety were the most common manifestations of mental impediment.

While male caregivers judged themselves to be in relatively good health (both physically and mentally), they nevertheless found caregiving to be a physically taxing experience. These same caregivers reported only moderate levels of life satisfaction in regard to their personal circumstances.

5
Contributions to Care
from the Outside

This chapter presents data characterizing the structure and function of the external support network that influences the male caregiver–elder care recipient dyad. Both informal (such as family) and formal (such as community service) systems of care were considered in terms of the roles they played in shaping the caregiving experience. These data are based on survey responses and interviews from support group leaders and male caregivers. Where possible, we present comparisons between these two respondent groups.

Structure and Function of the Informal Support Network: Male Caregiver Perceptions

Male caregivers were asked a series of questions about their past and current levels of caregiving effort and the recipients of that effort. Other questions addressed the structure of the caregiver's informal support network. Table 5–1 summarizes these data.

As shown, approximately two of every three males were providing care to spouses. An additional 12 percent were sons assisting mothers. Ten respondents were providing care to fathers. Less frequently, respondents identified the targets of their caregiving to be parents-in-law, friends, and siblings.

Data indicated that respondents had been performing their caregiving functions for considerable periods of time. More than

Table 5–1
Male Caregivers' Assessment of the Structure of the Informal Support Network

		Number	Percentage
Target of caregiving			
Spouse		109	67.7
Mother		19	11.8
Father		10	6.2
Mother-in-law		8	5.0
Father-in-law		5	3.1
Friend		5	3.1
Brother		3	1.9
Sister		2	1.2
	Total	161	100.0
Length of caregiving experience			
Less than one year		6	4.1
One to two years		26	17.8
Two to three years		18	12.3
Three to four years		25	17.1
Four to five years		24	16.4
More than five years		47	32.3
	Total	146	100.0
Level of caregiving responsibility			
Primary/major		126	87.5
Secondary		18	12.5
	Total	144	100.0
Number of persons sharing caregiving responsibility			
None		53	35.8
One		29	19.6
Two		36	24.3
Three		10	6.8
Four		10	6.8
Five or more		10	6.8
	Total	148	100.0
Frequency of family assistance in caregiving			
Very often		33	22.8
Sometimes		35	24.1
Seldom		46	31.7
Rarely/never		31	21.4
	Total	145	100.0
Extent of caregiving involvement			
Less than 10 hours a week		16	11.1
10–20 hours a week		20	13.8
21–30 hours a week		13	9.0
31–40 hours a week		9	6.3
41–50 hours a week		7	4.9
51–60 hours a week		5	3.5
More than 60 hours a week		74	51.4
	Total	144	100.0

95 percent of the sample who responded to this question indicated that they had been caregivers for more than one year. Almost two-thirds of the men had been caregivers for three years or more, with one in three performing in this capacity for more than five years. And the vast majority of these men had been serving as the primary or major caregiver during this time. Almost nine in ten respondents characterized their role in this manner.

Elder caregiving consumed substantial amounts of time in the lives of the survey respondents. More than half of the men said they provided in excess of sixty hours of caregiving during the course of the average week. Approximately one third reported their caregiving involvement levels at thirty hours or less.

In line with findings from other research (Horowitz & Dobrof 1982; Johnson & Catalano 1983; Stoller & Earl 1983), our data on family assistance patterns reflected uneven levels of help from relatives. Actually, a slight majority of respondents reported family assistance to occur only "seldom" or "rarely." Thirty-three (23%) men reported accepting family assistance "very often" while almost one in four men (24%) received moderate levels of assistance.

Table 5–1 reports that slightly more than one third of the respondents were sole providers of care. An additional 44 percent indicated having one or two persons bearing some of the responsibility of care. It was unusual for there to be more than two other persons sharing the caregiving experience. These men indicated that the most common sources of supplementary assistance were recipients' spouses, sons, and daughters. It is worth noting that the sons of recipients were mentioned more frequently than daughters as supplementary sources of aid, a pattern also reported by Rathbone–McCuan and Coward (1985). Although this finding is surprising in terms of traditional gender patterns in caregiving, it echoes Barusch and Spaid's (1989) conclusion that caregivers in their study tended to turn to children of the same gender for support. Less frequently mentioned persons who carried some responsibility for the care of the recipient were caregiver spouses, recipient daughters-in-law, recipient sisters, recipient sons-in-law, recipient granddaughters, recipient grandsons, and recipient nieces.

Male respondents were also asked whether they felt there were certain persons who should carry some of the caregiving responsibility but did not at the time of the survey. More than a third of the male respondents felt this was indeed the case. Daughters and sons were separated out in this respect. They were mentioned 33 percent and 29 percent of the time, respectively. Sisters, brothers, and daughters-in-law of the care recipients were mentioned moderately often. Grandsons, friends, granddaughters, and nephews were mentioned least often. It would appear that caregiving is perceived to be an immediate nuclear family affair.

The Structure of the Informal Support Network: Leader Views

Support group leaders were asked a series of questions concerning their observations of the experiences of male participants in their groups. Their responses were based on observations of 585 male support group members. The majority of men who participated in these groups provided care to spouses. A smaller proportion were sons caring for parents. Other relationships, such as men helping siblings, friends, and other relatives, were described only infrequently. Furthermore, leaders found that male caregivers were not likely to have more than one additional person available to help them during the course of caregiving.

The experience of caregiving for men in these support groups appeared to be as intensive an experience in the eyes of group leaders as it was to male caregivers themselves. Eighty percent of the group leaders found that male support group members were likely to have face-to-face contact on a daily basis with the persons to whom they provided care. Only one in ten group leaders found that male caregivers saw their care recipients less than three times a week.

Leaders also proved to be in close agreement with the men concerning the extent to which the latter felt there were other people who should be providing care, but did not. One in three leaders thought the men in their groups felt this way. Similarly, a majority of the leaders were convinced that their male group members did not feel they carried too much of the burden of care.

Needing and Using Community Services

Two indices were developed especially for this study to measure the range and intensity of formal community services received and needed by elder care recipients according to their male caregivers. (See appendix A for a complete description of these indices.) The Service Receipt Index is a 12-item measure that gauged the extent to which the older person benefited from a variety of formal gerontological services in addition to those received from relatives. A Service Need Index was also constructed. It contained the same set of community agency services found in the Service Receipt Index but was used to assess the extent to which caregivers perceived their elders to be in need of this repertoire of formal programs. Both indices are scored on a 2-point scale where a 0 indicates the nonreceipt or lack of need for the service and a 1 indicates the service is currently received or needed.

Table 5–2 summarizes male caregiver respondent scores on both the Service Receipt and Service Need Indices. As shown, both formal service receipt and service needs levels were relatively low, a finding at odds with other research, suggesting that male caregivers receive comparatively high levels of outside assistance with their tasks (Hlavaty 1986; Horowitz 1985a; Johnson 1983; Snyder & Keefe 1985). In all cases, mean item scores fell below the midpoint (.50) on the 2-point scale. More likely than not, elder care recipients, according to their male caregivers, were not receiving a wide range of agency services, nor would they have made use of them if they were available. This held true for services delivered in the older person's home as well as those which were available at congregate sites. Elders were most likely to receive visiting nurse, home health aide, adult day care, and friendly visitor or telephone reassurance services. They were least likely to utilize physical therapy, homemaker, and counseling services.

Table 5–2
Item and Index Scores for Service Receipt and Service Need Indices

Type of community service	Services currently received		Services needed		t value
	Mean	S.D.	Mean	S.D.	
Homemaker services	.04	.19	.40	.49	−4.70***
Home health aide services	.14	.35	.35	.48	−2.11*
Friendly visitor/telephone reassurance	.12	.33	.33	.47	−2.48*
Transportation/escort services	.09	.28	.17	.38	−1.27
Home-delivered meals	.10	.30	.18	.39	−1.16
Senior citizen center services	.11	.31	.17	.38	−0.90
Adult day-care services	.13	.34	.26	.44	−1.77
Counseling services	.06	.24	.26	.44	−3.13**
Physical therapy services	.02	.14	.31	.47	−4.56***
Visiting nurse services	.15	.36	.35	.48	−2.14*
Information and referral services	.11	.32	.16	.37	−0.63
Hospital services	.09	.29	.14	.35	−0.70
Summary index score	.10	.12	.16	.22	−1.45

Item and index matrix scores = 0–1, where higher score indicates service is more likely to be received or needed.
  *Statistically significant at $p < .05$
 **Statistically significant at $p < .005$
***Statistically significant at $p < .001$
S.D. = standard deviation

The services that stood out as being most needed were home-maker, visiting nurse, home health aide, friendly visitor or telephone reassurance, and physical therapy services. Elders were perceived to be least in need of hospital services, information and referral, senior center programming, transportation or escort, and home-delivered meals.

Comparative analysis of pairs of identical items in the two indices confirmed that needs for formal services exceeded their actual use. In every case, service need levels were higher than service utilization levels. These differences reached statistical significance in the case of homemaker services, physical therapy services, counseling services, friendly visitor or telephone reassurance services, visiting nurse services, and home health aide services. Summary index scores reflected the same pattern but did not achieve statistical significance.

Group leaders concurred in terms of the low service usage described by the men. Almost two of every three leaders indicated that no more than "several" of their male group members benefited from the assistance of community agencies. Group leaders were also asked to specify the most commonly used and needed community services by the men in their support groups. They specified adult day care, home health aide, homemaker, and information and referral services as those most frequently used. Homemaker, home health aide, and adult day-care services were also perceived to be those services which were most frequently needed but were not necessarily available. The least-used and the least-needed service according to group leaders was physical therapy. Group leaders believed that friendly visitors were also infrequently used.

In summary, then, male caregivers tended to minimize the extent to which they would use a wide range of services were they to be available—a tendency also displayed among the men in Vinick's (1984) sample. Nevertheless, they indicated that they were not receiving adequate supports from the formal service network. Group leaders concurred with caregivers by highlighting the need for certain traditional in-home services (that is, homemakers, home health aides) as well as congregate-based adult day-care services. With the exception of adult day care, all these services would provide men with ongoing support for rather than time away from their caregiving duties. These preferences reflect those of the men in Motenko's (1988) study who also preferred ancillary services that enabled them to carry on rather than providing respite time. Perhaps like the men in Miller's (1987) sample, our respondents wanted to remain in control, extending customary roles of authority at home and at work. This possibility finds support from comments made by several men interviewed in the local sample. When asked what made caregiving easier for him, one gentleman cited not outside help but his mother's dependency: "At times she's aware that she must rely on me. I feel good about that." Another man said that, even when home health aides assist with the care of his 85-year-old wife who has Alzheimer's disease, "I don't leave when they come. I make sure they treat her right." A few other local caregivers did mention elder day care as helpful, but they were in the minority.

Table 5–3 summarizes the relationship between service receipt, service need, and a series of survey measures discussed in chapter 4. Perceived need for service was not significantly associated with male caregiver financial health or life satisfaction. More importantly, it did not correlate with the care recipients' physical health status (as measured by the Illness Index), their capacity to perform activities of daily living (as measured by the ADL Index), or their degree of mental impairment (measured by the Behavioral Orientation Index). Put differently, elder recipients of care who were severely impaired (physically and mentally) as well as functionally disabled were no more likely than their healthier counterparts to benefit from the interventions offered by community service agencies. It would seem that male caregivers in combination with other informal providers of care were picking up the slack, becoming increasingly burdened by the demands of long-term care.

Other data in table 5–3 confirm that the deteriorating status of elders was accompanied by increments in the men's perceptions of the need for community assistance with caregiving responsibilities. Relatively strong positive correlations were discovered between the Service Need Index and both the Illness Index and the Behavioral Orientation Index. Furthermore, decrements in the male caregiver's financial health were accompanied by increases in the need for outside assistance. It would appear that, even though male caregivers testified to the increased need for outside assistance as the status of their care recipients deteriorated, they were not likely to have those needs satisfied.

There were no significant differences in the extent to which services were utilized when comparing spousal to nonspousal caregivers, employed to unemployed caregivers, and primary to secondary male caregivers. On the other hand, it is surprising to

Table 5–3

*Correlation Coefficients for Service Receipt and Service Need
and Selected Study Indices*

	Service Receipt Index	Service Need Index
Financial Health Index	−.05	.28*
Illness Index	.11	.58***
Activities of Daily Living Index	.06	.05
Behavioral Orientation Index	−.06	.43**
Life Satisfaction Index	.05	−.15

*p < .05
**p < .01
***p < .001

find that those caregivers who lived with their recipients of care reported significantly higher levels of community service usage than their counterparts who did not live in the same household as their recipients of care. Additional analyses confirmed that the gender of the care recipient, whether the elder had Alzheimer's disease, the age of the caregiver, and the overall health of the caregiver were not associated with different levels of community service utilization. Nor was the age of the care recipient or the extent to which other family members assisted with caregiving associated with changes in the level of community service usage.

Similar analyses performed on the Service Need Index confirmed that this same set of caregiver–recipient profile variables was generally not associated with differences in the caregiver's perceptions of service need. Only when the perceptions of spousal and nonspousal caregivers were compared did significant differences emerge. Specifically, spousal caregivers perceived significantly lower levels of need for outside assistance than did their nonspousal counterparts, a finding that parallels that of other recent research suggesting that when husbands are primary caregivers, the likelihood of supplementary assistance declines (Tennstedt, McKinlay & Sullivan 1989). On the other hand, as in the case of service receipt, such variables as caregiver age, overall health of the caregiver, level of caregiver responsibility, sex of the care recipient, and whether or not the recipient had

Alzheimer's disease were not associated with differences in levels of perceived need for community assistance. It is worth noting that the need for outside assistance expressed by employed caregivers proved to be considerably higher than that registered by unemployed or retired men; but it fell short of statistical significance.

Caregiver Support and Community Service Receipt

The level of caregiver responsibility (that is, primary versus secondary) and whether or not the caregiver–care recipient dyad utilized community services were subjected to a special analysis. Specifically, we examined the extent to which these variables were associated with differences in scores on selected other study indices and respondent profile variables.

There were no differences in the male caregivers' financial health, or the care recipients' Illness Index, ADL Index, and Behavioral Orientation Index scores when controlling for level of male caregiver responsibility. Nor did differences emerge when comparing primary versus secondary caregiver assessments of care recipient overall health and overall mental health. However, it was discovered that those men who designated themselves as primary caregivers reported significantly lower levels of life satisfaction. Primary male caregivers also reported their ages to be significantly higher than secondary male caregivers (69 years compared to 57 years), and rated their overall health, overall mental health, and functional health as significantly lower. It would thus appear that those male caregivers who could less easily assume the role of primary caregiver were nevertheless more likely to do so. A finding that is difficult to explain is that primary male caregivers provided help to persons who were significantly younger than those cared for by their secondary counterparts (73 and 81 years, respectively).

The characteristics of male caregivers and their elder care recipients were not found to vary in relation to receipt of community services, save for the latters' capacity to perform activi-

Table 5-4
Correlation Coefficients for Caregiving Support Variables and Selected Study Indices and Profile Variables

Indices/Variables	Hours devoted to caregiving each week	Amount of help provided by other family members	Length of caregiving experience	Number of people serving as secondary caregivers
Indices				
Financial Health Index	.14*	−.11	.10	.07
Illness Index	−.19*	−.02	.09	.03
Activities of Daily Living Index	.20*	.06	.43***	−.03
Behavioral Orientation Index	.14	.15*	.10	−.01
Life Satisfaction Index	−.02	.03	−.03	−.02
Profile Variables				
Age of care recipient	−.36***	.09	−.06	.06
Overall health of care recipient	.08	−.01	−.15*	.04
Overall mental health of care recipient	.16*	−.18*	−.21**	−.16*
Age of caregiver	.25***	.09	.14*	−.12
Overall health of caregiver	.20**	−.15*	.11	−.10
Overall mental health of caregiver	.22**	−.13	−.02	.00
Functional limitations of caregiver	.08	−.08	.17*	−.12

*p < .05
**p < .01
***p < .001

ties of daily living. Thus, recipient ADL limitations were found to be significantly greater for those male respondents who indicated they were in receipt of community services. On the other hand, male caregiver financial health, life satisfaction, age, overall health, overall mental health, and functional status did not significantly vary when comparing receipt and nonreceipt of community services. Nor did the care recipients' Illness and Behavioral Orientation Index scores, their age, overall health, and overall mental health vary when comparing those who were in receipt of formal community supports to those who were without them. Thus, older people's functional capacity, rather than their physical or mental health, emerges as a key variable in the utilization of community agency services.

Table 5–4 presents correlation coefficients for four key caregiving support variables and selected study indices and profile variables. Of particular interest here are such measures of caregiving support as the number of hours devoted by men to caregiving each week, the amount of help provided by other family members, the length of the men's caregiving experience or "career," and the number of people who served as secondary or supplementary caregivers. As shown, increasing amounts of time devoted to caregiving by men were associated with decrements in their self-assessed financial health, overall health, overall mental health, and increases in their age. Increments in time were also correlated with decrements in recipient mental health and functional capacity. More difficult to understand were significant negative associations between time devoted to caregiving and both the age of the care recipient and Illness Index scores.

It was revealing to find that increments in the frequency of family assistance were associated with decrements in the care recipients' level of behavioral orientation and overall mental health. While family members were found to be involved on a more frequent basis during the course of the older adult's mental and emotional decline, the absolute number of family members who engaged in more frequent periods of assistance declined. This pattern parallels that found by Stoller (1983, 1985) who concluded that, as elder caregiving stretches into chronicity, it becomes a drama cast with fewer and fewer players. For our respondents, a declining number of family members remained loyal to their caregiving tasks during the older adult's period of mental deterioration but those who did remain connected were providing increased measures of subsidiary aid.

Finally, it should be noted that the male's caregiving career was apparently accompanied by increased demands on their time and energy. In particular, longer term careers were witness to declining care recipient health (as measured by the Illness Index), mental health, and overall health, as well as deteriorating caregiver functional capacity. In terms of caregiving requirements, these correlations suggest that the demand for male caregivers to engage in active helping behaviors increased in tandem with declines in their own capacities.

Summary

The majority of men participating in this research were providing care to their spouses. Smaller proportions of men indicated the recipients of their care to be their mothers and fathers. Men had engaged in the caregiving enterprise for relatively long periods of time (three years or more in most cases) and committed substantial allotments of time to the effort—more than half provided in excess of sixty hours of care each week.

According to both males and group leaders, family assistance patterns were uneven. Men were not likely to have more than one or at most two additional family members helping them with caregiving. Many received no assistance whatsoever. Care recipient spouses, sons, and daughters were the most likely providers of supplementary help. Even so, a substantial proportion of male caregivers were convinced that certain members of the informal support network could have provided more help than they offered. In particular, they singled out sons and daughters of care recipients. It is clear that caregiving was characterized by help provided by immediate relatives—it was a family affair.

Male caregivers reported using relatively few community

services. More likely than not, they performed their caregiving functions without the assistance of the formal community service network. Community service need levels were also relatively low, though perhaps reflective of some degree of unsatisfied demand on the part of these men and their care recipients. Greatest need was expressed for in-home support services (such as homemaker services, visiting nurses, home health aides, and friendly visitors). Group leaders added adult day-care services to the "needs" list when given the opportunity to voice their opinion.

The need for outside intervention increased as the care recipients' health status deteriorated. Yet, there was some question as to whether these needs were actually satisfied by agency assistance. More frequently, it seemed, male caregivers simply assumed greater responsibility, and received assistance from select members of the immediate family. The men in this study did not present themselves as frequent users of formal care. They appeared to restrain their usage even as their own health and functional status were on the decline. Whether motivated by male stoicism, a desire to retain control, or gratification derived from sustaining a meaningful relationship, most of these men were going it alone or had minimal help from others. This pattern suggests that those planning policies, programs, and services for male elder caregivers should emphasize forms of assistance that support rather than replace their primary roles.

6
What Do Male Caregivers Do?

What types of caregiving tasks did the men in our study perform most frequently? What factors acted as barriers to their performance of these tasks? How competent did they feel as caregivers, and how satisfying was the experience? What stresses and burdens did they confront? And what were their perceptions of the appropriate gender allocation of caregiving tasks? The literature on gender roles suggests that men could be expected to more frequently and comfortably perform the practical, instrumental tasks of caregiving while eschewing personal care and the expressive dimensions of companionship and emotional support. Some of the findings reported in this chapter affirm this stereotypic conception of male caregiving; others challenge it.

Task Frequency

To assess the frequency with which men in this sample performed various caregiving tasks, the study questionnaire completed by caregivers included a Task Frequency Index. (See appendix A for a complete description of this index.) As seen in table 6–1, these male caregivers reported performing a wide variety of tasks with moderate frequency. Interestingly, they cited tasks related to providing companionship and emotional support as those most frequently performed. For example, one man from the local sample reported, "I provide her with a sense of well-being and some life enjoyment." Another viewed providing "a loving relationship" as his primary activity. The high frequency assigned to this activity appears to challenge the traditional view of men as unexpressive and emotionally detached (O'Neil 1982). It may bear out, however, the suggestion that men in middle and late life become more focused on affective connectedness and nurturance (Gutmann 1987; Solomon 1982). Horowitz (1985b) found that emotional support was the most common caregiving role for both men and women in her large sample—its salience may transcend gender. Many of the men in our local Delaware Valley sample who cited other tasks also mentioned companionship, or "just being there," as dimensions of their caregiving. This perception was mirrored in the views of some local recipients. As one 80-year-old woman receiving care from her son said, "He is companionship, and I'd be all alone without him, at dinner and so on." Another, also referring to a son, declared, "He does everything for me—but the best is that he loves me."

Factor IV, the Social Support task factor comprised of providing companionship and emotional support plus two others—help with paying bills or writing checks and help with writing letters and filling out forms, emerged as dominant in the men's ratings of the most frequently performed tasks. In fact, comparison of this factor to the other three factors revealed that caregivers reported performing social support tasks more frequently than tasks comprising any of the other three factors. As seen in the "Factors" section of table 6–1, the difference between the score for Social Support tasks and that for the next most frequently performed tasks—those of Instrumental Daily Living— was a statistically significant one. At first, it seems anomalous that help with paying bills and assistance with writing letters or filling out forms combined with companionship and emotional support to form the Social Support factor. But, in fact, the sharing of financial information and details of correspondence reflects a high level of trust, personal exposure, and intimacy characteristic of substantial interpersonal closeness.

Instrumental Daily Living tasks include marketing or shopping, cooking, doing the laundry, serving as an escort to the doctor's office, helping with medications, and doing home repairs—many of which fit into the traditional view of male

Table 6–1

Frequency With Which Male Caregivers Perform Caregiving Tasks
(Task Frequency Index)[a]

Tasks	Mean	S.D.	Rank
Providing companionship/emotional support	2.76	.59	1
Help with paying bills/writing checks	2.70	.84	2
Marketing or shopping	2.54	.82	3
Help with writing letters/filling out forms	2.43	.92	4
Escorting to doctor's office	2.41	.97	5
Help with legal matters	2.31	.99	6
Laundry	2.29	1.14	7
Preparing meals	2.26	1.17	8
Household cleaning	2.23	1.10	9
Home repairs	2.22	1.21	10
Help with medications/injections	2.02	1.31	11
Arranging for outside services	1.97	1.16	12
Help with dressing	1.83	1.30	13
Help with eating meals	1.73	1.31	14
Help with grooming	1.72	1.23	15
Help with telephoning	1.63	1.25	16
Help with bathing	1.61	1.37	17
Speaking for at community agencies	1.54	1.14	18
Help with going to the bathroom	1.44	1.23	19
Help getting in and out of bed	1.41	1.33	20
Supervising help provided by paid workers	1.35	1.32	21
Supervising help provided by relatives/friends	1.23	1.23	22
Summary index score	1.96	.74	

							t values			
Factors	Mean	S.D.	Rank	I × II	I × III	I × IV	II × III	II × IV	III × IV	
IV Social Support Tasks	2.65	.66	1	7.47*	5.96*	−6.61*	−0.77	−10.87*	−12.54*	
I Instrumental Daily Living Tasks	2.18	.91	2							
III Case Management Tasks	1.66	.88	3							
II Functional Daily Living Tasks	1.60	.87	4							

[a]Score Range = 0–3, where 0 = never, 1 = rarely, 2 = sometimes, and 3 = often
*$p < .001$

caregiving. Several of the local caregivers spoke of their activities as primarily instumental. Typifying this group was a 70-year-old man caring for his 85-year-old mother-in-law: "I take her on shopping trips; and I'm the taxi man to church and nearby family. And I remind her to take her meds." Similarly, a 76-year-old man caring for his wife who had Alzheimer's disease described his tasks as transportation, cooking, laundry, and housework.

Supervising the help of relatives or paid assistants, arranging for outside services, help with legal matters, and other tasks associated with case management were reported less frequently than either social support tasks or instrumental daily living tasks. This low frequency of case management tasks may be related to the men's general tendency to use little outside caregiver assistance. Finally, and predictably, functional daily living tasks such as help with going to the bathroom, assistance with bathing, dressing, and grooming, help with getting in and out of bed, and other aspects of personal care were reported with least frequency. Since most of these men were caring for women, this finding is not surprising and appears to support the traditional view that men do keep their distance from caregiving tasks involving physical intimacy. Nevertheless, those men providing personal care were doing it all. Many from the local sample talked about providing help with toileting, bathing, dressing, grooming, and feeding. One gentleman caring for his 75-year-old wife with Alzheimer's disease spoke of his tasks as though he were a parent caring for an infant: "I change her, feed her, and put her to bed." A 79-year-old man also caring for a wife with Alzheimer's listed his tasks thus: "I feed her and take care of her feeding tube three times a day. I turn her [in bed] four or five times a day. I empty her catheter."

Other men also spoke of performing specialized nursing-type skills. One man spoke of spending an hour each evening percussing his 75-year-old father's back to loosen phlegm from his lungs and then putting him on a ventilator. Another was in charge of changing his mother-in-law's colostomy bag. Here are men who appeared to press through whatever discomfort they might have experienced to provide the basics of intimate care.

The men's age did not appear to be a significant factor in the literal frequency with which they performed various caregiving tasks; this frequency was the same whether they were caring for a man or a woman. Moreover, neither being employed nor receiving community services made a difference in task frequency. There was some evidence that men in the worst health were providing more assistance than those physically more able to do so.

Task frequency was greater in the substantial group of caregivers caring for people believed to suffer from Alzheimer's disease than in the group whose care recipients were not thought to have Alzheimer's, reflecting the increased overall caregiving demands of people with organic brain syndromes. As expected, those men who lived with the person they cared for and those who saw themselves as primary caregivers reported performing more caregiving tasks than those who lived apart from the care receiver and considered themselves secondary helpers. As the focus narrows to the dyadic, spousal family nucleus, in other words, the number of caregiving tasks climbs.

It is interesting to note that caregiver support group leaders reported that most male caregivers in their groups were neither retiring from their jobs nor reducing their number of hours at work to fulfill their caregiving responsibilities. Nearly three-quarters of the leaders reported that none of the men in their groups had retired or cut back work hours; another 14 percent reported that only one of their group members had done so. Since there was a high proportion of retirees in the sample, this finding may mean that many men entered support groups having already retired. Nevertheless, comments from respondents in the local sample reveal that some men had retired in order to increase the time they had available for caregiving. As one 63-year-old former insurance salesman taking care of his mother noted, "It's become my lifestyle. I left my job to do it—[I] couldn't do both. I took up a new ministry." Moreover, for those 10 to 15 percent of the men who were not cutting back to accommodate caregiving, it is likely that they were, like Brody's (1981) "women in the middle," juggling many competing demands.

Male Caregivers' Competence

Using the same list with which they rated task frequency, male
caregivers assessed their level of competence on the Task Competence Index. (See appendix A for a detailed description of this
index.) The four major factors described in the discussion of the
Task Frequency Index apply here as well. They are: (I) Instrumental Daily Living tasks; (II) Functional Daily Living tasks; (III)
Case Management tasks; and (IV) Social Support tasks.

As seen in table 6–2, the men saw themselves as quite competent. As a man from the local sample caring for his 84-year-
old sister put it, "Nothing scares me!" Another, caring for his
mother who had Alzheimer's disease, boasted that he could do
"whatever has to be done. I've been shown how to do everything and I can do it all." A look at specific kinds of tasks,
however, reveals considerable variation. Specifically the men felt
most competent performing those tasks associated with social
support.

In this instance, however, it was the top-rated social support
task of paying bills and writing checks, together with a fairly
high rating for help with writing letters and filling out forms,
that put the social support factor in first place. Providing companionship and emotional support, reported previously as the
most frequently performed activity, ranked in only eighth place
in terms of the men's feelings of competence. Apparently they
felt more competent doing something more concrete than providing emotional support—a pattern that reflects traditional gender
conceptions of male competence. Nevertheless, a few men in the
local sample felt that they shined in this affective arena. One 65-
year-old man taking care of his mother felt most competent
"being her son [and] giving her a feeling of being loved." And a
man caring for his wife who had Alzheimer's disease believed he
did best at "holding her hand (and) talking to her."

But most caregivers in the national sample gave themselves
higher competence ratings on transportation, help with telephon-
ing, home repairs, shopping, and other instrumental tasks. They
felt less competent as case managers. One man, however, felt
being a man gave him an edge in this area.

"I have more guts than my sisters. I stood up to a social

Table 6–2
Caregivers' Reported Degree of Competence in Performing Caregiving Tasks (Task Competence Index)[a]

Tasks	Mean	S.D.	Rank
Help with paying bills/writing checks	2.88	.35	1
Escorting to doctor's office	2.77	.51	2
Help with telephoning	2.67	.59	3
Help with writing letters/filling out forms	2.57	.61	4
Home repairs	2.51	.73	5
Marketing or shopping	2.48	.63	6
Help with legal matters	2.46	.66	7
Providing companionship/emotional support	2.44	.65	8
Arranging for outside services	2.40	.73	9
Help with medications/injections	2.35	.92	10
Laundry	2.30	.81	11
Speaking for at community agencies	2.27	.89	12
Supervising help provided by paid workers	2.26	.85	13
Help with eating meals	2.21	.91	14
Help getting in and out of bed	2.18	.96	15
Supervising help provided by relatives/friends	2.13	.92	16
Preparing meals	2.11	.91	17
Household cleaning	2.10	.84	18
Help with going to the bathroom	1.85	1.10	19
Help with dressing	1.83	1.04	20
Help with bathing	1.79	1.10	21
Help with grooming	1.69	1.07	22
Summary index score	2.30	.49	

						t values			
Factors	Mean	S.D.	Rank	I×II	I×III	I×IV	II×III	II×IV	III×IV
IV Social Support Tasks	2.63	.36	1	7.10**	2.18*	−5.63**	−4.46**	9.38**	6.45*
I Instrumental Daily Living Tasks	2.44	.52	2						
III Case Management Tasks	2.31	.62	3						
II Functional Daily Living Tasks	1.96	.87	4						

[a]Score Range = 0–3, where 0 = not competent at all, 1 = not very competent, 2 = somewhat competent, and 3 = extremely competent

*$p \geq .05$

**$p \leq .001$

worker when my mother had her stroke and refused to put her in a nursing home. My sisters wouldn't have done that."

Predictably, the men experienced least competence giving the personal care that sex-role socialization has assigned to women in this culture. In fact, only one respondent in the local sample felt most competent providing personal care. Several in this group who reported overall competence made exceptions when it came to functional tasks. One believed he could do everything well, "up to incontinence." A local caregiver looking after his 74-year-old sister felt skilled at everything but feeding her. When asked what tasks they felt least competent performing, the local group most frequently cited personal care. Repeatedly they mentioned help with bathing, dressing, feeding, and dealing with incontinence as tasks to which they brought least skill.

Comments by recipients of these men's care echoed their sentiments. One woman, for example, said her son "can do anything except personal things." Another declared, "At bathroom needs, women are better." But she then qualified her statement by saying, "My husband is an exception; he is at ease with these things and so am I." One local recipient said that "men are less helpful with hands-on help the first time, but they get better." This and other comments by both local caregivers and recipients suggests that men's sense of competence may be compromised by sex role socialization that affords them little training in personal care. One man believed that this might change:

> Most women have raised children and have more practice in caring for someone. Today, however, if both husband and wife work, both spend equal time raising the kids. These men will then have had more of the experience of caring when they have to care for the elderly.

An examination of the association between competence and several other factors revealed that neither the men's general health, their age, nor their employment status made a difference in their overall sense of caregiving competence. Single men appeared to feel as competent as those who were married. Employment status made no difference, nor did being a primary versus being a secondary caregiver. Interestingly, the men's sense of competence did not vary in relation to the length of time they had been attending caregiver support groups, suggesting that membership in such a group does not necessarily help men feel that they are doing a better job.

Men caring for women felt as good at what they were doing as those who were caring for men; and those whose recipients were receiving community services felt no less competent than those without such assistance. Whether the recipient had Alzheimer's disease or not made no statistically significant difference, nor did living with the recipient. A sense of competence appeared tied more to men's subjective perception of the kind of job they were doing rather than to contextual factors. One particularly articulate woman with a degenerative muscle disease summed up her husband's areas of competence in ways that reveal its multiple dimensions:

> He is good at physically righting me and getting me around. He is good at dressing me. He has become a very good cook. He is a good housekeeper when he wants to be—when people are coming to visit; day-to-day housekeeping is not so good. He's particularly good at respecting my intelligence and treating me like an adult. He treats me like an equal partner on important issues that concern us both.

Male Caregivers' Level of Satisfaction in Caregiving

That a feeling of competence is not always associated with satisfaction is revealed by the caregivers' ratings on the Task Satisfaction Index. (See appendix A for a detailed description of this index.)

Findings displayed in table 6–3 suggest that, in general, the tasks associated with caregiving were only "not very" to "somewhat" satisfying for these men. As one local caregiver put it, "It's part of my life. I'm used to it. I get tired of doing it, but . . . ." Most satisfying were those tasks associated with social support; but here, the provision of companionship and emotional support, not paying bills and writing letters, rated highest.

Table 6–3
*Caregivers' Reported Degree of Satisfaction
in Performing Caregiving Tasks
(Task Satisfaction Index)[a]*

Tasks	Mean	S.D.	Rank
Providing companionship/emotional support	2.33	.80	1
Home repairs	2.23	.77	2
Help with paying bills/writing checks	2.14	.94	3
Help with legal matters	2.10	.83	4
Escorting to doctor's office	2.07	.86	5
Marketing or shopping	2.06	.87	6
Help with medications/injections	2.04	.88	7
Preparing meals	2.03	.92	8
Help with eating meals	2.00	.93	9
Help with writing letters/filling out forms	1.92	.86	10
Speaking for at community agencies	1.91	.83	11
Arranging for outside services	1.91	.89	12
Laundry	1.83	.85	13
Help with telephoning	1.82	.95	14
Help with grooming	1.80	.95	15
Help getting in and out of bed	1.75	1.00	16
Supervising help provided by paid workers	1.70	.92	17
Help with dressing	1.70	.98	18
Household cleaning	1.58	.88	19
Supervising help provided by relatives/friends	1.58	.94	20
Help with bathing	1.57	1.00	21
Help with going to the bathroom	1.43	1.09	22
Summary index score	1.93	.63	

						t *values*			
Factors	Mean	S.D.	Rank	I×II	I×III	I×IV	II×III	II×IV	III×IV
IV Social Support Tasks	2.22	.76	1	1.63	2.23*	−2.86**	−.55	−3.41***	−4.32**
I Instrumental Daily Living Tasks	2.06	.66	2						
III Case Management Tasks	1.82	.72	3						

Table 6–3 continued

				t values					
Factors	Mean	S.D.	Rank	$I \times II$	$I \times III$	$I \times IV$	$II \times III$	$II \times IV$	$III \times IV$
I Functional Daily Living Tasks	1.70	.77	4						

Score Range = 0–3, where 0 = not satisfying at all, 1 = not very satisfying, 2 = somewhat satisfying, and = extremely satisfying

$*p \leq .05$
$**p \leq .01$
$**p \leq .001$

The response of one Delaware Valley gentleman taking care of his 84-year-old mother was typical. He felt most satisfied "just being together. She used to like to be with me, and now she has me for hours!" Another reported most satisfaction taking care of his elderly sister "when I make her laugh, hug her, and get her dancing!" It is interesting that this activity was both the most frequently performed and the most satisfying to these men; yet, as revealed in the previous section, it was not the one they felt most competent performing.

The overall satisfaction rating for social support tasks was significantly higher than that for the group of activities rated as next most satisfying, that is, those associated with instrumental daily living. A few men in the local sample, however, did cite instrumental tasks as most satisfying, especially cooking. One who was taking care of his 76-year-old wife said, "When I see her enjoy her food, I'm happy." More typical was another care-giver's response, who found "cooking dinner every night" his least satisfying task: "Sometimes I don't feel like eating but I have to make dinner anyway." A few seemed to enjoy providing transportation to appointments or for recreation.

Supervising help provided by others, arranging for outside services, and other aspects of case management rated third in overall satisfaction. And, as expected, the men found least satis-faction in giving personal care, especially toileting. To an open-ended question about what kinds of help they found least satisfying, the caregivers in the local sample mentioned changing beds, changing diapers or pads, managing incontinence, changing

colostomy equipment, and other functional tasks most frequently.

Clearly, for some, the accumulated tasks of caregiving ex-
acted a high personal toll. As one local respondent caring for his
75-year-old father confided, "I'm pretty dissatisfied . . . . After
all these years it's amazing I haven't thrown in the towel. My
dad is really hard to care for and is manipulative at times. I feel
I can't do any more and I'm afraid something will happen. My
chest hurts and my heart pounds." Apparently reluctant to give
such explicit voice to their dissatisfaction, several others expressed the resigned acceptance embedded in the phrase, "It
could be worse . . . ."

The men's satisfaction with their tasks was related neither to
the recipients' age nor to their level of education. Similarly, the
caregivers' age, level of education, and general health were not
associated with the degree of satisfaction their tasks brought
them. Interestingly, the number of other persons sharing some
responsibility for caregiving made no measurable difference in
the frequency, competence, or satisfaction with which these male
caregivers performed their tasks. While it may have had other
benefits, the presence of others in the helping network appeared
not to related to the men's perception of the job they were doing.

Barriers to Caregiving

Men do not go about their caregiving tasks unimpeded. To determine which barriers compromised male caregiving specifically,
we asked both the men in our sample and the leaders of caregiver support groups to complete a Barriers to Caregiving Index
(see appendix A for a detailed description). As summarized in
table 6–4, the problems associated with recipients' mental and
emotional health appeared to act as the primary barrier to the
amount of caregiving provided. This barrier was rated highest by
both caregivers and by support group leaders. This and other
barriers such as the caregivers' and recipients' general physical
health, the stress associated with caregiving, and the nature of
the recipients' personality comprised the Physical/Emotional

Health factor and was rated highest by both caregivers and leaders—higher to a statistically significant degree than the other two factors we examined.

The primacy of this barrier was given voice by many men in the local sample. For some, their own health posed a major problem. Several men in the local sample cited chronic fatigue or physical limitations like heart problems or a bad back that made it hard to turn or lift recipients. Others mentioned recipients' health problems, especially incontinence, when asked about barriers to their efforts. One man caring for his severly disabled wife who had frequent incontinence exclaimed, "It takes too much time! If it were just the Alzheimer's, I could do it standing on my head!"

But for most local respondents, recipients' emotional health and related personality disturbances—"the mental stuff," as one respondent termed it—appeared to impose the most formidable barriers. One man caring for his 81-year-old wife with Alzheimer's reported: "Sometimes she has a mind of her own. She won't get up, and I get mad and frustrated. I shouldn't, but . . . ." Another gentleman found his sister's "sarcastic, arguing" attitude hardest to deal with. Still another complained because his wife who had severe dementia "won't cooperate with me to put medicine on her arm and leg rashes four times a day, so I gave up. She scratches till it bleeds; it's very distressing." Expressions of anger were difficult for several local men. One man caring for his wife who had Alzheimer's disease was clearly managing considerable frustration: "When she gets her back up I'm lost. You can't belt her, so you just walk around and sweat." For others, the generational role reversal was most difficult. As one man caring for his demented mother commented, "I'm the parent and she's the child!" Another experienced conflict about "ordering her [his 88-year-old mother] around."

The group of barriers rated next in importance by caregivers was that related to gender. These barriers included their opinion of what appropriate male behavior should be as well as their perception of others' opinions of appropriate male behavior. A man helping care for his 75-year-old mother-in-law reported, "She will not accept physical help from me—only from her

Table 6-4
Caregivers' and Leaders/Organizers' Reports of the Degree to Which Various Barriers Limit
the Amount of Caregiving
(Barriers to Caregiving Index)[a]

Barriers	Caregivers			Leaders/Organizers		
	Mean	S.D.	Rank	Mean	S.D.	Rank
Stress of caregiving	1.73	.98	1	1.92	.84	1
Recipient's mental/emotional health	1.45	1.18	2	1.89	.93	2
Recipient's physical health	1.27	1.14	3	1.76	.94	4
Recipient's general personality	1.12	1.09	4	1.76	.97	3
Quality of past relationship with recipient	1.05	1.25	5	1.61	1.05	5
Caregiver's general health	.97	1.04	6	1.53	.86	6
Availability of relatives/friends who can help	.95	1.01	7	1.47	.95	7
Availability of community services	.94	.96	8	1.37	.88	8
Family's tradition of helping others	.78	1.03	9	1.32	1.00	9
Nature of caregiver's social life	.75	.90	10	.80	.84	14
Caregiver's opinion of appropriate male behavior	.75	1.06	11	.78	.78	15
Requirements of caregiver's job	.73	1.02	12	1.10	1.10	10

Table 6–4 Continued

Barriers	Caregivers			Leaders/Organizers		
	Mean	S.D.	Rank	Mean	S.D.	Rank
Family obligations	.68	.94	13	1.00	.92	11
Others' opinions of appropriate male behavior	.68	.99	14	.61	.70	16
Gender of recipient	.53	.94	15	.84	.84	12
Geographic distance from recipient	.38	.81	16	.82	1.08	13
Summary index score	.91	.58		1.31	.60	

	t values			t values		
	I × II	I × III	II × III	I × II	I × III	II × III
	8.36*	8.20*	.55	16.00*	7.97*	6.84*

Factors	Caregivers			Leaders/Organizers		
	Mean	S.D.	Rank	Mean	S.D.	Rank
I Physical/emotional health	1.25	.73	1	1.73	.71	1
III Gender related	.74	.75	2	.76	.62	3
II Community/family support	.71	.58	3	1.22	.74	2

aScore Range = 0–3, where 1 = minimally, 2 = to some degree, and 3 = very much so

*p ≤ .001

daughter." And a young man caring for his great aunt said, "I can't help her in the shower. She wouldn't like me to see her if she got into trouble showering." One 66-year-old single man caring for his 94-year-old mother felt impeded because he was "taking care of a woman. Not having been married, I don't do well with things like getting her dressed." Another regretted that his gender interfered with his "doing the feminine things my mother would enjoy."

Female recipients of male elder care tended to agree with the caregivers. One woman whose husband cared for her, for example, thought he was effective "except for bathroom needs—there I'd prefer a woman."

Rated least in importance were Community/Family Support barriers such as the requirements of the caregivers' job, availability of friends and relatives or community services, and the nature of family obligations. These logistical barriers loomed as less important than those that were subjective and relational. Men from the local sample rarely mentioned jobs or family obligations as an issue that got in the way of their caregiving. And even those who mentioned family obligations spoke about relational aspects. One young man who had helped care for his mother-in-law, now deceased, reflected: "She wanted me out of the way. Our relationship became a battle for my wife's attention." Several others felt that caregiving imposed barriers to other aspects of their lives rather than vice versa. One gentleman helping care for his wife's parents, both demented, summed up the sentiments of many: "My time is not my own. My wife and I liked to do activities outside the home before." Another man who was single and taking care of his 85-year-old mother said, "It has limited me socially. I can't meet anybody. She resents it when people come over. I can't include her in everything, so I don't bring anybody over."

One barrier not included in the list presented to the national sample—finances—was mentioned by several men in the local group. In one example, a 74-year-old woman with Alzheimer's disease had forgotten to pay her taxes for four years. Her brother was trying to pay them off in addition to buying adult diapers, medicines, and other supplies. Others said simply: "There's not enough money!"

An examination of the possible association between barriers to caregiving and a range of other variables—that is, the recipients' gender, receipt of community services, and whether or not the elder had Alzheimer's disease; and the caregivers' age, marital status, employment status, and his distance from the recipient—turned up no statistically significant correlations. Again, these pragmatics seemed less important than relational issues.

Although agreeing with caregivers that Physical/Emotional Health barriers were most limiting to caregiving, the support group leaders differed in their ranking of barriers comprising the other two factors. They believed that Community/Family Support barriers ranked second, whereas Gender-related barriers were perceived to be least limiting. We have no way of determining whether the leaders were underestimating the importance of gender barriers or whether the caregivers were minimizing barriers associated with community and family support.

Caregiver support group leaders' ratings of the overall degree to which barriers limited the caregiving efforts of their group members did not differ to a statistically significant degree in relation to their gender, whether or not they had been caregivers themselves, and whether or not they had received special support group leadership training. However, female leaders were more likely than their male counterparts to report that gender-related factors acted as barriers to male caregiving. It may be that they were more sensitive to gender issues than male leaders were.

Perhaps most striking is the finding that the leaders consistently rated the *degree* to which various barriers impeded caregiving as greater than did the caregivers themselves. The difference between overall summary index scores for the two groups was statistically significant. Statistically significant differences between these respondent groups also appeared in their Physical/Emotional Health factor scores and in their Community/Family Support factor scores. Only in Gender-related factor scores was there no statistically significant difference. It seems unlikely that the leaders would overestimate the degree to which various barriers got in the way of the caregiving rendered by men in their support groups. More likely is the possibility that the caregivers themselves minimized or denied the extent to which various barriers impeded their efforts.

The Stress and Burden of Caregiving Tasks

Though believed to be less subject to caregiving burden than women (George 1984; Barusch & Spaid 1989; Young & Kahana 1989), men are not immune. Asked to rate the tasks of caregiving according to the degree of burden associated with them, the men in our sample cited hands-on personal care as burdensome most frequently, echoing their perceptions of the tasks they found least satisfying and at which they felt least competent. Helping with legal and financial matters was mentioned moderately often as were case management tasks and household chores (one of the instrumental aspects of daily living). The provision of emotional support and companionship, shopping, transportation, and dealing with behavioral problems were rarely mentioned as stressful.

When support group leaders were asked to report which caregiving activities their male group members found most stressful, they were in accord concerning the apparent stress associated with personal care. In contrast to the male caregivers themselves, however, the leaders perceived the provision of emotional support and companionship as more stressful than case management tasks. Similarly, when asked to report which dimensions of providing care seemed most satisfying to their male group members, they appeared to ascribe little satisfaction to the emotional and affectional benefits of caregiving—a perception at odds with that of the men themselves. The fulfillment of marriage vows or other family obligations was most frequently cited as being satisfying to men in their groups, whereas the successful performance of caregiving duties was cited only half as often.

This latter finding is interesting when viewed from the perspective of Gilligan's (1982) work on male and female moral development. As applied to caregiving, Gilligan's formulations suggest that women would approach their tasks from an ethic of caring, while men would be motivated primarily by an ethic of justice and obligation—"doing the right thing," in other words. Although previously reported findings suggest that many men in this sample appeared to be motivated by an ethic of caring, the leaders seemed to suggest that the fulfillment of vows and obligations was most satisfying. Indeed, a few men in the local sample mentioned this dimension. As one gentleman put it, "It's the absolute right thing to do—the only thing." Another man taking care of his 81-year-old wife with Alzheimer's disease declared, "I don't mind in the least. It's an obligation: I think I should." But the possibility exists that the caregiver support group leaders may have been influenced by a stereotypic view of what men *should* find most satisfying. Those men in the local sample frequently expressed some combination of an ethic of caring and an ethic of justice. One man said, "She's my wife, and I love her." Another saw caregiving as "a way to pay honor to my mother"; and another reflected, "I've been married to her for so long. I still love her. She was the perfect mate for me." Perhaps, as the literature on men's emotional expression suggests (O'Neil 1982; Winogrand et al. 1987), male caregivers may not talk as much in support groups about the emotional and affectional benefits of their caregiving as they do about other dimensions of caring.

Sex Role Perceptions of Caregiving

Since gender appeared to play a role in men's experience of barriers and burdens associated with their caregiving tasks, we asked them to respond to a number of tasks in terms of whether a man, a woman, or either should perform them. As in previously described indices, the items identified as Instrumental Daily Living tasks, Functional Daily Living tasks, Case Management tasks, and Social Support tasks provided an organizing structure for these data. In general, the men's ratings reflected an androgynous perception of appropriate task allocation, with most caregivers believing that either a man or a woman should perform many tasks. Marked differences did appear, however, and these differences fell along traditional gender lines.

Table 6–5 reveals that 52 percent thought men should do

Table 6–5
Frequency With Which Male Caregivers Indicated
Whether a Man, a Woman, or Either Should
Perform Various Caregiving Tasks

Tasks	A woman should help		Either a man or a woman should help		A man should help	
	Number	*Percentage*	*Number*	*Percentage*	*Number*	*Percentage*
Home repairs	3	2.6	53	45.3	61	52.1
Help with paying bills/writing checks	4	3.3	94	77.7	23	19.0
Help with legal matters	3	2.5	96	81.4	19	16.1
Escorting to doctor's office	10	6.6	89	73.6	22	18.2
Help with writing letters/filling out forms	6	4.7	107	84.3	14	11.0
Speaking for at community agencies	5	4.1	105	86.8	11	9.1
Providing companionship/emotional support	11	8.8	98	78.4	16	12.8
Marketing or shopping	13	10.6	92	74.8	18	14.6
Arranging for outside services	9	7.3	102	82.3	13	10.5
Help with telephoning	6	5.2	104	89.7	6	5.2
Supervising help provided by relatives/friends	9	7.9	96	84.2	9	7.9
Supervising help provided by paid workers	12	11.0	86	78.9	11	10.1
Help with eating meals	18	15.1	86	72.3	15	12.6
Household cleaning	20	16.0	87	69.6	18	14.4
Help getting in and out of bed	21	18.8	77	68.8	14	12.5
Laundry	21	16.9	91	73.4	12	9.7
Preparing meals	22	17.9	88	71.5	13	10.6
Help with medications/injections	16	13.6	95	80.5	7	5.9
Help with going to the bathroom	42	36.8	59	51.8	13	11.4
Help with dressing	48	38.4	60	48.0	17	13.6
Help with grooming	47	38.5	63	51.6	12	9.8
Help with bathing	46	40.7	55	48.7	12	10.6

home repairs, while only 2.6 percent thought that women should do them. Similarly, 16 percent of the caregivers thought that men should provide transportation to the doctor's office, while only 7 percent thought women should do this job. Gender allocation of tasks traditionally performed by women was more stereotypic, however. For example, only 11 percent of the caregivers thought that men should help prepare meals, whereas 18 percent thought women should do this. Similarly, only 10 percent thought men should do laundry; 17 percent thought this was women's work.

These distinctions were even more marked in examining the men's responses related to personal care. Here the traditional gender role allocation remained fixed. Thirty-seven percent of the caregivers thought that a woman should help with going to the bathroom, whereas only 11 percent thought that a man should assist in this task. Similarly, although 10 percent of the caregivers thought that a man should help with bathing, four times as many thought that a woman should do so. The ratio was similar for help with grooming.

In terms of social support tasks, 19 percent of the caregivers believed that men should help with paying bills and writing checks; only 3 percent of them thought that a woman should do so. Similarly, 11 percent thought that men should help with writing letters and filling out forms, whereas only 5 percent thought women should help with this. Consistent with findings reported elsewhere in this chapter, 13 percent of the men thought that men should provide companionship and emotional support in contrast to 9 percent who thought that women should do so.

The least apparent gender differences appeared in relation to case management tasks. For example, the number of caregivers who thought that a man should supervise help provided by friends, relatives, or paid assistants was identical to the number who thought that a woman should. The largest difference appeared in relation to assistance with legal matters, where 16 percent of the respondents thought that a man should help as opposed to 3 percent who thought that women should help. In general, case management tasks appeared to be viewed as gender neutral.

Relationships among Task Experience Measures and Other Study Variables

Table 6–6 displays correlations among the three major task experience indices, as well as correlations between these indices and other previously reported indices. As shown, there was a significant association between the frequency with which caregiving tasks were performed and the level of competence experienced in doing them. But, generally, frequency was related neither to the level of satisfaction experienced in caregiving nor to barriers to caregiving. Predictably, there was a fairly strong correlation between task frequency and the level of assistance the recipients required in the activities of daily living; the more help the recipient required, the more frequently men performed caregiving tasks.

Table 6–6
Pearson's Correlations Between the Experience Indices and Other Study Indices[a]

	I	II	III	IV	V	VI	VII	VIII
I	—							
II	.39***	—						
III	.03	.46**	—					
IV	.13	.10	.03	—				
V	.16	.10	−.25	.31**	—			
VI	.24	.31*	−.00	.28	−.11	—		
VII	.42***	.09	−.08	.05	.06	.05	—	
VIII	.17*	−.02	−.09	.23**	−.06	.44**	.21**	—

a   I = Task Frequency Index
   II = Task Competence Index
   III = Task Satisfaction Index
   IV = Barriers to Caregiving Index
   V = Service Receipt Index
   VI = Service Need Index
   VII = Activities of Daily Living Index
   VIII = Behavioral Orientation Index
   *$p \leq .05$
   **$p \leq .01$
   ***$p \leq .001$

The more competent men felt at caregiving, the more satisfaction they experienced, as would be expected. More difficult to explain is the statistically significant positive correlation between the level of competence experienced in caregiving and the extent to which gerontological services would be used if available. Perhaps the high levels of care required by recipients who needed more services led to high levels of competence in those caring for them. Barriers to caregiving such as job responsibilities, family obligations, and the stress of caregiving were associated with higher levels of received services. This finding suggests that more outside services were used in situations where male caregivers experienced more barriers to fulfilling their caregiving responsibilities.

Barriers to caregiving were also associated with higher levels of behavioral and mental disturbance in recipients. There was also an association between increased behavioral difficulty and the frequency with which caregiving tasks were performed, an increased need for services, and, to a smaller degree, an increased need for assistance with activities of daily living. Such behavior as uncooperativeness, withdrawal, agitation, and suspiciousness clearly taxed these male caregivers in a number of ways.

The extent to which leaders reported that their group members experienced barriers to caregiving was related to their reports of the frequency with which male caregivers had face-to-face contact with the care recipients, the number of caregivers in their groups who thought others should help them out but did not, and the number who felt they carried too much of the caregiving burden. Expectedly, the strongest correlation emerged between leaders' estimates of the number of their male group members who felt others should be helping them provide care and the number who felt they carried excessive burden.

Summary

The male caregivers we surveyed were performing a wide range of tasks associated with elder caregiving, from hand holding to home repair. In contrast to the stereotype that male caregiving is primarily instrumental in nature, these men's responses suggested that, overall, the tasks associated with social support were those they performed most frequently, most competently, and with the greatest degree of satisfaction. Ranked second in degree of frequency, competence, and level of satisfaction were instrumental daily living tasks, followed by case management tasks and, in last place, the "hands-on" functional aspects of personal care.

The examination of barriers to caregiving experienced by these men also revealed a focus on the relationship dimension of their tasks. Both the caregivers themselves and the leaders of caregiver support groups reported that the recipients' mental and emotional health appeared to be the primary barrier to the amount of caregiving men provided. The caregivers' responses suggested that gender-related factors ranked next in importance as caregiving barriers. Their own and others' opinions of what appropriate male behavior should be appeared to be related to the amount of caregiving they provided, while the availability or unavailability of community and family supports ranked last in importance as a barrier. Caregiver support group leaders, on the other hand, believed gender factors to present fewer barriers than the availability of family and community support. Consistently, however, the leaders rated the degree to which most barriers impeded caregiving as greater than did the caregivers themselves. This discrepancy suggests the possibility that, like the men in Vinick's (1984) study, these caregivers may have minimized the barriers to their tasks.

The majority of caregivers and leaders cited assistance with going to the bathroom, bathing, grooming, and other functional tasks of daily living as those most burdensome and stressful. Although only a few caregivers reported that providing emotional support and companionship was most stressful, the leaders believed that this caregiving activity was more stressful for their male group members than case management or other tasks. In addition, the leaders reported that men in their groups got more satisfaction from fulfilling vows and obligations than from emotional and affectional aspects of caregiving. This perception, undocumented by what the men themselves reported, is in line with Gilligan's (1982) conclusion that men are motivated primarily by an ethic of justice and obligation rather than by an ethic of caring.

The male caregivers' attitudes toward the appropriate gender allocation of caregiving tasks reflected considerable androgyny. When respondents clearly indicated that one sex or another should perform certain tasks, however, most thought that women rather than men should assist with personal care. As might be expected, most thought men rather than women should help with home repairs, transportation, and other instrumental aspects of daily living. Consistent with other study findings, most who divided tasks along gender lines thought that men rather than women should perform various social support tasks.

7
Family Relationships and the Male Caregiver

An understanding of the tasks of male caregivers, although crucial, reveals only one dimension of their caregiving experience. Bowers (1987) points out that a sole focus on tasks fails to capture the interpersonal and intrapsychic issues that make up the invisible work of caregiving. Elder caregiving occurs in the context of an interpersonal relationship, and the nature of this relationship inevitably affects—and is affected by—the caregiving situation. Since elder caregiving relationships usually have a substantial impact on overall family life, it is important to explore family reactions to the caregiving situation. In this chapter we report findings related to the degree of allegiance between caregivers' and recipients' family members, family members' attitudes toward the care being provided, and the extent of support and assistance other family members provide.

Findings reported in previous chapters suggest that the social and emotional support dimension of caregiving was of overriding importance to male caregivers in this sample. A more focal examination of some of the relationship dynamics between caregiver and recipient, therefore, is crucial. To this end, we also report findings related to the degree of intimacy, affiliativeness, and affection between male caregivers and the recipients of their care.

Strength of Relationships and Degree
of Allegiance in the Caregiver's Family

Male caregivers in this sample completed a Familism Index on which they rated the extent to which a number of statements about family allegiance applied to their own families. (See appendix A for a detailed description of this index.) They responded on a scale that ranged from 1 ("not at all") to 3 ("very much so") to statements intended to tap such issues as filial responsibility, collaborative family decision making, and feelings of moral obligation.

The overall level of family allegiance reported was only moderate. A statement regarding the family's feeling of responsibility to be with parents in times of illness received the highest mean rating, followed by a statement referring to the family's willingness to share their homes and a statement that family members share as many activities as possible. These ratings appear to be consistent with the kind of strong family affiliation that would lead to a decision to provide elder family caregiving to a relative in need.

The statements receiving lowest ratings were those associated with the family's vulnerability to outside influences on its political views, the feeling of moral obligation to pay other family members' medical bills, and the geographical proximity of family members. These latter statements seem to deal with pragmatic rather than affective aspects of family life and are, perhaps, further from the relationship "core" of the family than are the more highly rated statements.

The men's perceptions of the level of allegiance in their families appeared unaltered in relation to a wide variety of potentially influential factors including their age, their health, whether they remained employed or were retired, or whether or not they saw themselves as primary caregivers.

Interestingly, single male caregivers reported significantly higher levels of family allegiance than did those who were married. This finding suggests the possibility that unmarried male caregivers were closer to and more allied with their extended families than were those whose primary relationships were with a spouse.

Responding to a series of open-ended questions about closeness and loyalty in their immediate families, 85 percent of the respondents in the local Delaware Valley sample reported high levels of allegiance. As one man caring for both his parents put it, "There's so much love in this family; that's what keeps us going."

All but five of the 30 local men reported that family members felt a sense of loyalty to each other. Often this loyalty was expressed by nuclear family members, especially children. Even though they lived far away, children who telephoned or visited from time to time were viewed as loyal and helpful. One man believed his family expressed their loyalty through their confidence in him: "My family trusts me to administer all the finances. I write all the checks!"

This rosy portrait of family allegiance faded, however, when the local caregivers talked about their extended families. Sixty-five percent reported little closeness. A few said this had to do with geographic distance; but several mentioned emotional estrangement as well. As one gentleman said about his family, "each is very separate and concerned about himself."

Almost 70 percent of the caregiver support group leaders rated male caregivers' overall family relationships as good; another 17 percent rated them as excellent. Similarly, their ratings of the caregivers' families' attitudes toward the care being provided were relatively high. Thirty-two percent believed families to be very supportive, and another 58 percent thought them to be somewhat supportive. Neither ratings of the quality of family relationship nor the level of support differed to a significant degree in relation to whether or not the leaders themselves were or had been elder caregivers, whether or not they'd had special support group leadership training, or whether they were men or women.

Positive perceptions of family relationships were reflected in ratings made by the caregivers themselves. Asked to rate their families' attitude toward the help they were providing to their elder care recipients, 65 percent rated their families as very supportive, and another 21 percent thought them to be somewhat supportive. These ratings did not differ to a statistically significant degree in relation to the recipient's gender, whether or not he or she received outside assistance, or whether or not he or she had Alzheimer's disease; nor in relation to the caregiver's marital status, employment status, or whether or not he considered himself carrying major caregiving responsibility.

The perception of men in the local group corroborated the positive view of family support portrayed by respondents in the national sample. Responding to a question about the care they were providing, all the men but one believed their families approved. As one man put it, "They're happy that I do it and tell me all the time that I do a nice job." Another remarked, "They seem very pleased—my brother says, 'I don't know how you do it!' "

Others mentioned feeling supported; but some believed family reactions were ambivalent. As one mused, "They consider the care to be excellent; but there's some resentment about prolonging his [grandfather's] life and preventing inheritance."

A few others reported that either their families or the care recipients themselves were concerned about their well-being. One man caring for his 80-year-old mother with Alzheimer's disease said of his family, "They know I'm doing the best I can. They want me to take care of myself so I don't get run down." Another respondent commented, "My mom said she didn't bring me into this world to do this. She gets really depressed. It's getting harder for her to bear what I do."

Such sentiments were expressed by one of the recipients being cared for by her 52-year-old son: "I don't like imposing on him or bothering him. Sometimes I try to avoid asking him to do things for me." These issues notwithstanding, the majority of local men, like those in the national sample, were providing elder care in a supportive and affirming family context.

Caregivers also rated the quality of their families' relationship to the recipient of care; 47 percent rated this relationship as excellent, and another 30 percent rated it as good. Those caregivers who were unmarried rated the quality of family relationship to the recipient as significantly better than did those who were married. Possibly, the unmarried caregivers were caring for a parent or sibling toward whom other family members might have greater affinity than they would for an in-law. It is interesting to note that the ratings of families' relationships to care recipients did not vary in relation to the elder recipient's gender, whether or not the recipient lived with the caregiver, whether or not he or she received outside assistance, or had Alzheimer's disease. Neither did these ratings change in association with whether or not the caregiver believed himself to carry major caregiving responsibility.

Did these generally affirming and supportive family attitudes find expression in concrete assistance? To find out, we asked the male caregivers to rate the frequency with which family members provided direct assistance to the recipient. On a scale where 1 = "rarely or never" and 4 = "very often," the mean rating was only 2.5 (standard deviation (S.D.) = 1.1). Almost half the sample (47 percent) reported that their families provided assistance only "seldom" or "rarely or never," and only just over one in five caregivers believed they received family help "very often." Comments by the care recipients in the local sample corroborated this unevenness in assistance. Two of those nine who could be interviewed mentioned infrequent help by a sister. One woman said her granddaughter and daughter-in-law assisted "on occasion"; and another woman said her son helped out "sporadically." More frequent secondary assistance came from neighbors, caregivers' girlfriends, or paid personnel. One 84-year-old woman receiving care from her 71-year-old brother bristled when asked about this: "Nobody helps us. The neighbors stink. Nobody cares, and I've been in this house 70 years!"

The recipient's gender, and whether or not he or she received community assistance, lived with the caregiver, or had Alzheimer's disease appeared to make no difference in male caregivers' ratings of family assistance levels. Neither did the caregiver's marital status nor whether or not he thought himself to carry major responsibility alter these ratings.

Clearly positive family attitudes, while undoubtedly supportive, did not always translate into actual helping efforts. The modest levels of family assistance found here are in line with results from other research suggesting that, for the most part, elder caregiving is a dyadic enterprise (Horowitz & Dobrof 1980; Johnson & Catalano 1983; Stoller & Earl 1983).

The Nature of the Caregiver-Recipient Relationship

It is important, therefore, to look specifically at dimensions of the relationship between the caregiver and the recipient of his care. An examination of caregivers' responses to a number of true—false statements about their relationship with the persons they cared for suggests that they tended to meet many recipients' dependency needs while having few of their own met. Most male caregivers (93 percent) reported that the persons they cared for relied on them more than they were able to rely on the recipients. Sixty-four percent reported that they were asked for advice by the recipients more than they sought advice from them. Less than 10 percent reported that they could call on their care recipients for help in decision making, and only 5 percent reported that the recipients made decisions in which both they and the caregivers were involved. Although only 16 percent reported that they always did as the recipient said, 60 percent responded "false" to a statement that they won arguments with their care recipients most of the time, suggesting that, although they may have ultimately prevailed in interpersonal issues, caregivers paid a price in related tension and conflict. This finding lends support to Horowitz and Shindelman's (1983) conclusion that the increased dependency of elders may bring the caregiving dyad closer emotionally but makes interactions less gratifying for the caregiver. This seemed especially true for men in the local sample who were caring for relatives with dementia. As one man caring for his wife remarked, "She doesn't realize I'm doing all this care. Once in a while she says my name, so she must know who I am . . . ."

To explore the degree of perceived caregiver—recipient reciprocity, we asked the caregivers to rate five forms of behavior in terms of how frequently the recipients initiated them (as measured by the Recipient Affection index) and how frequently the caregivers initiated them (as measured by the Provider Affection index). As seen in table 7–1, caregivers reported that care recipients initiated affectionate behavior with relatively low frequency. The ranking reveals that "listens to what is being said" received the highest rating while "asking how the other is doing" received the lowest. When reporting on the frequency with which they, themselves, initiated various forms of affectionate behavior, the caregivers consistently reported that they initiated all of them with greater frequency. Highest ratings were reported for "shows concern," "listens to what is being said," and "asks how the other is doing." Interestingly, "displays physical affection," ranked second as behavior initiated by recipients, was ranked last as behavior initiated by the caregivers themselves. Across the board, however, the levels of frequency with which caregivers reported that they initiated affectionate behavior were higher to a statistically significant degree than the levels at which they believed recipients initiated it.

Table 7–2 summarizes the frequency with which both recipient-initiated and caregiver-initiated forms of behavior were

Table 7–1

Caregivers' Report of the Frequency With Which Recipients and Caregivers Initiate Affectionate Behavior (Affection Index)[a]

Behavior	Recipient Initiates			Caregiver Initiates			t value
	Mean	S.D.	Rank	Mean	S.D.	Rank	
Listens to what is being said	2.02	1.10	1	3.23	.81	2	−10.31*
Displays physical affection	1.98	1.23	2	2.73	1.04	5	− 7.22*
Shows concern	1.82	1.17	3	3.24	.76	1	−11.85*
Shows sympathy	1.71	1.21	4	3.09	.82	4	−11.28*
Asks how the other is doing	1.57	1.32	5	3.23	.88	3	−12.61*
Summary index score	1.86	.99		3.10	.67		−12.85*

[a]Score Range = 0–4, where 0 = rarely, 1 = seldom, 2 = sometimes, 3 = often, and 4 = almost always
*$p < .001$

Table 7–2

Means and Standard Deviations of Frequency With Which Recipients and Caregivers Initiate Affectionate Behavior, by Several Study Variables

	Recipient Initiates				Caregiver Initiates			
Variables	Summary Index Score Mean[a]	S.D.	t/F	Significance (p value)	Summary Index Score Mean[a]	S.D.	t/F	Significance (p value)
Recipients' gender								
Male	2.00	.58	0.76	.46	2.93	.59	−0.86	.41
Female	1.84	1.01			3.11	.67		
Alzheimer's disease								
Yes	1.72	.98	−3.59	.001	3.14	.65	1.11	.28
No	2.43	.82			2.97	.71		
Community services								
Yes	1.71	.95	−1.10	.27	2.90	.70	−2.34	.02
No	1.92	1.03			3.18	.59		
Living together								
Yes	1.94	.99	1.24	.22	3.04	.71	−1.73	.09
No	1.70	1.01			3.24	.57		
Care recipient								
Spouse	1.74	1.01	2.36	.02	3.20	.57	−2.19	.03
Nonspouse	2.18	.90			2.85	.85		

	Mean	SD		p	Mean	SD		p
Caregiver's employment status								
Employed	2.06	.98	1.31	.20	2.88	.84	−2.03	.05
Retired	1.78	1.01			3.22	.57		
Caregiver has primary caregiving responsibility								
Yes	1.87	1.03	1.43	.17	3.16	.62	2.56	.02
No	1.60	.58			2.55	.83		
Length of time in support group								
0–1 Year	2.26	1.04	6.00	.003	3.08	.81	.14	.87
1–3 Year	1.68	.95			3.15	.53		
3+ Year	1.56	.91			3.09	.61		
Caregiver's overall health								
Excellent	2.35	.96	5.58	<.005	2.98	.76	.64	.53
Good	1.77	.97			3.14	.61		
Fair to poor	1.57	.92			3.15	.71		
Caregiver's age								
36–64	1.88	.99	.05	.95	3.03	.77	1.01	.37
65–74	1.85	.88			3.19	.47		
75–84	1.81	1.16			3.01	.81		

[a]Score Range = 0–4, where 0 = rarely or never, 1 = seldom, 2 = sometimes, 3 = often, and 4 = almost always

reported. Frequencies differed to a significant degree in association with several study variables. For example, those recipients who did not have Alzheimer's disease were thought to have initiated more affectionate behavior than did those with Alzheimer's. Curiously, recipients initiated this behavior with those caregivers whose overall health was excellent more than they did with those whose health was only good or fair-to-poor. Perhaps healthier caregivers were more available and receptive to affection from recipients than were those whose health was poor. Those men who were members of caregiver support groups for less than a year reported higher levels of recipient-initiated affectionate behavior than did those who had been in support groups one or more years. It is likely that the levels of impairment in recipients whose caregivers had just begun attending support groups were less than those for recipients whose caregivers had been attending longer; the less impaired recipients were probably more able to be affectionate than were their more impaired counterparts.

In terms of the frequency of caregiver-initiated affectionate behavior, whether or not the recipient had Alzheimer's disease did not appear to make a difference. Those caregivers helping recipients who received community services, however, reported lower frequencies of initiating affectionate behavior than did those whose care recipients did not receive it. Getting outside help may have taken some of the pressure off them to be the initiators. Those providing care for a spouse reported that they initiated affection more frequently than did those caring for other relatives—an expected finding. More puzzling is the finding that, as recipients, spouses were perceived to initiate less affectionate behavior than nonspouses. Perhaps, ongoing affectionate behavior was so routine between spouses that it was less apparent to the caregiver than were instances where nonspouses were affectionate.

Finally, those caregivers who were retired reported providing more frequent affectionate behavior than did those still employed; probably being present at home and having more time available was related to increased levels of affection. And, predictably, those caregivers who viewed themselves as having primary responsibility for the care of the recipient reported higher frequency in initiating affection. On the whole, however, care-givers reported little reciprocity of affection between themselves and the recipients of their care. They were performing labors of love in a situation where this love was not always returned in the form of equivalent displays of caring and affection. Never-theless, several caregivers in the local sample believed that the recipients of their care appreciated what they were doing and were concerned about their well-being. Speaking about his 75-year-old wife who had Alzheimer's disease, one man declared, "I think she likes the idea. She tells everyone what a nice guy I am and that I do everything." Another, taking care of his aged mother, believed that, "In a way it puts her at ease; but in a way she feels it's a burden for me—that she's a bother and is stopping me from doing other things."

Several local care recipients validated this sentiment. One 84-year-old woman with a seizure disorder who was receiving care from her brother commented, "I think it's kind of hard. He should be more free—he's tied down with me." But there was some evidence that recipients rarely verbalized these feelings to their caregivers. As one woman put it, "We really don't talk about it much. We accept the status quo [and] don't overanalyze it."

The leaders of caregiver support groups were also asked to rate the degree of balance or "give and take" of concern and affection that generally existed between male caregivers and their care recipients. Thirty-four percent of the leaders thought that a fair amount of reciprocity was present in the relationships their group members had with their care recipients, and another quar-ter believed that there was a great deal of give and take. It appears that the leaders perceived more recipient–caregiver give and take than what the caregivers themselves experienced.

Male Caregivers' Feelings toward the Recipients of Their Care

In the face of providing caregiving in which the balance of reci-procity seemed uneven to them, how did these men feel about the persons they were caring for? When asked to rate a number of statements describing feelings toward their care recipients, their responses reflected that their relationships with the recipients were stable, close, and that they managed agreements and disagreements well. Lowest frequency ratings were associated with the two negative statements on the index—that is, those related to lack of trust and a poor relationship.

Those men who believed themselves to be primary caregivers tended to agree more frequently with positive statements about the recipients than those not carrying major responsibility; their ratings differed to a statistically significant degree. Beyond this, little else seemed to be associated with caregivers' overall positive feelings toward their recipients. There were negligible rating differences in relation to the recipient's gender, living arrangements, and to whether or not he or she had Alzheimer's disease. Neither did these ratings vary in relation to whether the caregiver was married or not, was employed or retired, nor in relation to his age, his overall physical health, and how long he'd been in a caregiver support group.

Caregivers rated their level of satisfaction with the amount of concern expressed for them by their care recipients on the Family Function Index (see appendix A for a detailed description). The caregivers gave highest ratings to statements reflecting satisfaction with the way they and their recipients spent time together and the way recipients responded to their feelings. Consistent with findings reported here previously, they gave the lowest ratings in response to a statement about the degree to which they could count on recipients for reciprocal discussion and for help in mutual problem solving.

Those caregivers with primary care responsibility reported significantly higher levels of satisfaction than did those who did not carry primary responsibility. Those who were retired also gave significantly higher satisfaction ratings than did those who remained employed. Perhaps in line with suggestions by Fitting and associates (1986) and by Horowitz (1985a), these men have found in caregiving a meaningful new role for retirement. Not surprisingly, those whose care recipients did not have Alzheimer's disease gave higher satisfaction ratings than did those taking care of Alzheimer's patients. Reported satisfaction levels did not differ, however, in relation to such variables as the recipient's gender, assistance from community services, or the caregiver's marital status; nor did they vary in relation to the caregiver's overall health or with his age.

Subjective Burden in Caregiving

Earlier we presented findings related to the degree of burden assigned to specific types of tasks by men in our study. As many authors point out, however, it is caregivers' subjective *experience* of burden—the cognitive and emotional changes accompanying stress and strain—that most compromises their sense of well-being (George & Gwyther 1986; Gwyther & George 1986; Morycz 1985; Zarit, Todd & Zarit 1986). To look at this dimension of burden for the men in our sample, we asked them to complete a Burden Index (see appendix A for a detailed description). Overall, these caregivers reported a relatively low burden score. As detailed in table 7–3, they reported feeling afraid of what the future holds for the recipient most frequently. Ranked second was a direct question about how often they felt burdened by elder caregiving. But they reported having these feelings only "sometimes." Lowest ratings were given to questions regarding a wish to leave the care of the recipient to someone else and one asking if they felt their recipients asked for more help than they needed. So, while these men viewed some aspects of caregiving as somewhat burdensome, they did not apparently believe that their recipients were making excessive demands, nor did they want to turn caregiving over to someone else.

It is not surprising that significantly higher burden scores were reported by men who were living with the recipients of their care than for those who were not. Also, those men who were combining caregiving and employment reported higher burden ratings than did those who were not. Whether they were caring for a man or woman made no difference in burden. Intuitively, it seems that those caregivers whose recipients were receiving community services and were free from Alzheimer's disease would report less burden; but neither of these factors

Table 7–3

*Male Caregivers' Reports of the Frequency With Which They Feel
Stress and Strain When Taking Care of Their Care Recipients
(Burden Index)[a]*

Questions	Mean	S.D.	Rank
Are you afraid of what the future holds for your relative/friend?	2.72	1.21	1
Overall, how often do you feel burdened in caring for your relative/friend?	2.01	1.16	2
Do you feel that, because of the time you spend with your relative/friend, you don't have enough time for yourself?	1.97	1.10	3
Do you feel stressed between caring for your relative/friend and trying to meet the responsibility for your family or work?	1.92	1.10	4
Do you feel that your relative/friend currently affects your relationship with other family members or friends in a negative way?	1.92	1.10	4
Do you feel uncertain about what to do about your relative/friend?	1.55	1.10	5
Do you feel your health has suffered because of your involvement with your friend/relative?	1.51	1.17	6
Do you feel you don't have as much privacy as you would like because of your relative/friend?	1.37	1.35	7
Do you wish you could just leave the care of your relative/friend to someone else?	1.15	1.17	8
Do you feel that your relative/friend asks for more help than he/she needs?	1.01	1.06	9
Summary index score	1.71	.77	

[a]Score Range = 0–4, where 0 = never, 1 = rarely, 2 = sometimes, 3 = quite frequently, and 4 = nearly always

were associated with a statistically significant difference. Similarly, the ratings did not differ significantly in relation to the caregivers' marital status, how long they'd been in a caregiver support group, their age, or whether or not they carried primary care responsibility. Levels of burden did vary in relation to the caregivers' health. As expected, those in "excellent" health reported significantly lower burden ratings than did those who characterized their health as only "good."

Interviews with caregivers in the local Delaware Valley sample rendered a more complex and sharply drawn version of burden than did the questionnaire results. Several of the men did worry about the fate of their care recipients. And phrases familiar to anyone who has ever worked with caregivers cropped up: One man referred to caregiving as "a downer," another spoke of it as "a pain in the neck." But some of the men were more pointedly outspoken about the negative impact of caregiving on their lives. As one respondent caring for his 91-year-old mother put it, "It's a hassle and a nuisance. I can't get away to travel or go away for even one day!" And, speaking about caring for his deceased mother-in-law, a 39-year-old man complained that caregiving "made me feel crazy. There is no corner of our lives that was not impacted. If it was [sic] physical caregiving . . . . but the mental drain was awful." Another man caring for a sister with Alzheimer's disease referred to himself "as a prisoner in my own home."

One man spoke of declining health associated with the strain of caring for his 82-year-old mother; and another confided, "It's made an older man out of me. I come home and do work, get up and do work . . . ." Still another man caring for his grandfather confessed that he was worn down by the feelings of responsibility and obligation and "resentful that the burden is placed on me. [I] would never do it again."

For several others, however, feelings of responsibility, obligation, and duty appeared to make the burden more bearable, to give it a context. This seemed especially true for those assisting spouses. As one gentleman put it, "My wife and I have been married 47 years. We've had a good life. It's the best I can do. If reversed, she'd do it for me." Another said, "It doesn't bother me. You get married; you make a vow for sickness and health . . . ." Another, caring for a wife with Alzheimer's disease, declared, "I don't mind in the least. It's an obligation; I think I should." These men appeared to view caregiving as part of a normative marital expectation, employing an ethic of justice (Gilligan 1982) that helped them cope.

For others caring for their wives, it was clear that they sought to fend off painful feelings of loss through caregiving.

One man said, "I thank God for the privilege, because when she goes . . . ." and dissolved into tears before he could finish his thought. Others spoke poignantly about the losses already sustained. Like the caregivers described by Moritz, Kasl, and Berkman (1989), these men appeared to be mourning lost companionship and intimacy. As one respondent whose wife had Alzheimer's disease confided, "You have no one to share things with any more. We used to go to restaurants together, do chores, and so forth. Now I'm by myself." Another mentioned feeling "lonely for my wife, my marriage, our relationship." These men had entered what Hlavaty (1986) refers to as a "limbo" marital status with a spouse "who, in a sense, has died leaving the body behind" (p. 3). As Motenko (1988) indicates, for such men stress and burden result not from caregiving per se, but from this sense of personal loss.

A substantial number of local men—both spousal caregivers and those caring for parents, in-laws, or other relatives—spoke of caregiving not as burdensome but as instructive, positively challenging, and growth promoting. One man caring for his 88-year-old mother said, "It has made me more sensitive about senior people. I'm a better person, and I apply my self-knowledge to other situations." Another, caring for both parents, declared, "It's made me as complete a person as I can be. It gives you all kinds of challenges and experiences." Another man was sustained in caring for his wife by "the love I have for her." And a gentleman summed up the feelings of many when he referred to taking care of his 96-year-old mother as a "labor of love—I love to make her happy."

While it is possible that these men were masking burden with defenses of reaction formation or denial, their genuine affection suggests that they were motivated by an ethic of caring (Gilligan 1982) and, like the subjects in Motenko's (1988) ethnography, had found personal gratification, pride, and meaning in their caregiving roles. As Liptzin (1984) concludes, "Masculinity does not exclude caring that may be growth enhancing and involves as much 'taking' or benefit to the 'care-giver' as to the 'care-recipient' " (p. 76).

Correlations among Caregiving Relationship Variables

An examination of the Pearson's correlations displayed in table 7–4 reveals some interesting relationships among the caregiving relationship variables. For example, the reported level of overall family concern and allegiance (the Familism Index) had a relatively strong positive correlation with the families' attitude toward the help the caregivers were providing for the recipients. An even stronger relationship appeared between the level of family allegiance and the families' relationship to the recipients—the stronger the allegiance, the better the relationship. The more family allegiance existed, the more frequently family members assisted with caregiving, and the less burden the caregivers reported. There was also a statistically significant correlation between the reported level of family allegiance and the level of caregivers' satisfaction with the concern expressed for them by the care recipients.

A strong positive association existed between the families' attitude toward the caregivers' helping efforts and how well the families got along with the older recipients. And, the better the families' attitude toward the caregivers' help, the more family members appeared to help out. Positive family attitude toward the caregiving efforts was related to lower levels of caregiver burden. Higher ratings of the families' relationship to recipients were positively correlated with the frequency with which they assisted caregivers, lower levels of reported burden, greater frequency of provider-initiated affectionate behavior, a greater degree of intimacy and affiliativeness in the caregiver–recipient relationship, and increased caregiver satisfaction with the help they received from recipients. Interestingly, the frequency with which family members helped out with caregiving was not related to the severity of caregiver burden; it can be speculated that family attitude more than literal helping efforts may have made a difference.

In order to pinpoint those factors that would best explain fluctuations in caregiver burden for the men in this study, a

Table 7–4

Pearson's Correlations Between Selected Caregiving Relationship Variables

	I	II	III	IV	V	VI	VII	VIII	IX
I Familism Index	—								
II Family's attitude toward caregiver's help	.63***	—							
III Family's relationship to recipient	.70***	.75***	—						
IV Frequency of family's help with caregiving	.63***	.49***	.53***	—					
V Burden Index	-.28***	-.27***	-.32***	-.02	—				
VI Recipient Affection Index	.09	.09	.09	.02	-.17*	—			
VII Provider Affection Index	.17	.13	.30***	.10	-.23**	.17*	—		
VIII Quality of Relationship Index	.15	.12	.28***	.07	-.37***	.38***	.36***	—	
IX Family Function Index	.23**	.17*	.21**	.24**	-.33***	.64***	.29***	.51***	—

$*p \leqslant .05$
$**p \leqslant .01$
$***p \leqslant .001$

series of previously described indices were entered into a stepwise multiple regression (see appendix C for further explanation). Specifically, the Barriers to Caregiving Index, the Quality of Relationship Index, the Behavioral Orientation Index, the Service Receipt Index, the Task Frequency Index, the Family Function Index, the Financial Health Index, and the status of living arrangements of caregiver and care recipient were treated as independent variables. Caregiver burden was considered the dependent variable in the equation. Table 7–5 summarizes the results. As shown, these variables accounted for 46 percent of variance in Burden Index scores. Each of these variables significantly predicted caregiver burden. However, in accordance with our correlational analysis, the relative quality of the caregiver's personal relationship with the family and with the care recipient proved to have the strongest impact on caregiver burden. A positive and intimate relationship with one's family served best to reduce the level of stress and burden expressed by these men. The intensity of psychological and social barriers to caregiving also had a major influence on burden levels.

Correlations between scores on the Burden Index and those of other relationship variables suggest how important emotional factors are in men's perception of stress in elder caregiving. Lower burden ratings were related to increased levels of affection

Table 7–5
Regression of Independent Variables on Caregiver Burden

Independent variables	beta	R^2	p
Quality of dyadic relationship	−.37	.14	.0000
Quality of family functioning	−.33	.11	.0003
Barriers to caregiving	.32	.10	.0006
Nonreceipt of community services	.28	.08	.01
Financial health of caregiver	.24	.06	.005
Frequency of task performance	.21	.05	.03
Cohabitation with care recipient	.22	.05	.009
Behavioral orientation of care recipient	.21	.04	.02
Total R^2		.46	

initiated by care recipients, increased affection initiated by the caregivers themselves, higher levels of caregiver–recipient intimacy and affiliativeness, and higher levels of caregivers' satisfaction with the degree of concern they received from recipients.

As might be expected, the more that care recipients initiated affectionate behavior, the more providers initiated it as well, although this association was weak. Similarly, increased recipient-initiated affection was correlated with the degree of reported intimacy and affiliation, and, most strikingly, with the degree of caregivers' satisfaction with the help they received from elder recipients. High ratings of provider-initiated affection were correlated with heightened intimacy and affiliativeness between caregiver and recipient and with levels of caregiver satisfaction with the help received from recipients. Finally, higher levels of intimacy and affiliation were related to a statistically significant degree to the caregivers' level of satisfaction with the help received from recipients. Not only do these correlations underscore the interwoven nature of many relationship variables; they suggest that, indeed, the measures of relationship were tapping various dimensions of the same construct.

Correlations between Relationship Variables and Other Study Variables

When examining associations between these relationship variables and previously reported study indices, we found levels of concern and allegiance among family members were positively correlated to a moderate degree with the level of satisfaction and competence the men experienced in performing caregiving tasks. This was particularly true in the case of instrumental tasks and personal care.

Expectably, higher levels of burden were associated with more frequent performance of caregiving tasks. This was particularly true for the frequency with which caregivers reported helping with instrumental tasks of daily living and social support tasks. Greater burden levels were also related to perceived barriers to caregiving; statistically significant correlations emerged between burden and physical and emotional health barriers, community and family support barriers, and, to a lesser degree, gender-related barriers. Higher burden ratings were correlated with increased receipt of community services, the presence of recipient health problems, and with higher levels of recipient behavioral and mental disturbance. Not surprisingly, there was a negative association between increased burden and reported levels of satisfaction in caregiving. Strongest correlations emerged between higher burden levels and decreased satisfaction in performing instrumental tasks of daily living and personal care. In other words, caring for those recipients in the poorest health, who needed a high level of community service assistance and evidenced cognitive and behavioral disturbance, was associated with higher levels of burden in these men. And the more burden they experienced, the less satisfied they felt.

The less difficulty recipients had with activities of daily living, the more they appeared to initiate affection with their caregivers. Similarly, lower levels of behavioral and mental disturbance were associated with increased amounts of affection initiated by recipients. Nevertheless the men's overall satisfaction in caregiving was not correlated with recipient-initiated affectionate behavior to a statistically significant degree.

The view of oneself as being affectionate and loving had substantive associations with many dimensions of male caregiving. When looking at the frequency of affection initiated by caregivers, we discovered statistically significant positive correlations with task frequency, task satisfaction, and task competence. Not surprisingly, those who saw themselves as most affectionate experienced most satisfaction and competence from providing companionship and other aspects of social support.

Caregivers also reported being more affectionate with recipients who needed fewer community services but who nevertheless needed more help with activities of daily living. Those reporting that they initiated more affectionate behavior also reported heightened levels of personal life satisfaction.

Congruent with this latter finding is the positive relationship discovered between higher levels of reported intimacy and affiliativeness between caregiver and recipient and increased satisfaction in caregiving. Stronger relationships were discovered between higher levels of affiliativeness and greater satisfaction in performing case management tasks, social support tasks, and instrumental daily living tasks. Only in relation to personal care did the correlation not reach statistical significance. This finding suggests that, although intimacy and affiliation may enhance male caregivers' satisfaction in performing most caregiving tasks, it may not ameliorate their dissatisfaction with assisting recipients with toileting, bathing, grooming, and other functional tasks.

Higher levels of caregiver–recipient intimacy and affiliation were associated with the caregivers' greater overall satisfaction with life. Predictably, increased intimacy and affiliativeness were also correlated with a lower reported incidence of barriers to caregiving, particularly those barriers associated to recipients' and caregivers' physical and emotional health. Predictably, there was greater intimacy and affiliativeness when recipients presented fewer behavioral disturbances and mental difficulties.

The caregivers' level of satisfaction with the concern for them expressed by recipients was closely related to the level of satisfaction they reported in caregiving. This held true regardless of the category of tasks carried out. The caregivers' satisfaction with caregiving appeared to be enhanced in a context where recipients were able to demonstrate their concern for helper well-being. This was also the case in relation to their sense of overall competence in performing caregiver tasks.

Not surprisingly, the more behavioral disturbances and mental difficulties displayed by elder care recipients, the less satisfied caregivers were with the concern expressed for them by the recipients. Similarly, the less the male caregivers felt that their recipients expressed concern for them, the more they believed mental and emotional health barriers impeded their caregiving. The salience of these difficulties was affirmed repeatedly.

The Perspective of Support Group Leaders

As support group leaders reported it, the better the overall relationship existing between male caregivers and their families, the more there existed affective reciprocity between caregiver and recipients. Similarly, better family relationships were associated with fewer perceived barriers to caregiving. As might be expected, the worse the overall family relationships, the more support group leaders thought that men in their groups felt others should be helping out and that they were carrying too much of the burden. Also, leaders' responses confirmed that improved family relationships were correlated with higher levels of emotional health in male caregivers. Similarly, their ratings suggested that those men providing caregiving in supportive family contexts experienced the load of their burden as lighter.

Summary

Overall, although the level of allegiance among members of male caregivers' families appeared to be only moderate, both the caregivers and the leaders of caregiver support groups believed families to be supportive of the caregiving these men were providing and felt that families had largely positive relationships with the care recipients. Families' positive and supportive attitudes did not necessarily translate into concrete assistance to the caregivers, however. Nearly half the male caregivers reported that their families helped out only seldom or rarely.

In terms of caregiver—recipient reciprocity, the caregivers believed that they provided more than they received, particularly in relation to satisfying dependency needs. In the give and take of affection, these men consistently rated themselves as initiating more affectionate behavior than their care recipients. Nonetheless, they reported largely positive feelings toward their care recipients as well as only low to moderate levels of caregiving stress and strain. A number of dimensions of the caregiver—recipient relationship were improved in the context of strong family allegiance, a positive family attitude toward the recipients, high levels of support for the caregivers' efforts, and increased frequency of actual concrete caregiving assistance from family members. With these family supports in place, caregivers reported higher levels of satisfaction with the amount of concern their recipients expressed for their well-being and higher levels of

intimacy and affiliativeness with the recipients. Both a positive
family context and positive caregiver—recipient relationships were
strongly associated with caregivers' reported competence and satisfaction in caregiving. Clearly, despite stereotypic conceptions
that might suggest otherwise, emotional and relationship factors
were of central importance to these men's experience. Findings
reported in this section suggest that these factors must be considered when planning and implementing programs, policies, and
direct services.

8
Men's Attitudes toward Helping Others

As important as relationship dynamics in male caregiving are the attitudes that men bring to this endeavor. How did the men in this sample view elder caregiving? What were their perceptions of the elderly? And, since elder caregiving has traditionally been viewed as women's work, how did they see themselves in relation to attributes that have become linked through socialization with male and female sex roles? Once again, these male caregivers believed emotional gratification to be an important motivating factor in caregiving, and they tended to view themselves as possessing many affective traits usually associated with the female sex role.

Male Caregivers' Attitudes toward Elder Caregiving

In order to assess the male caregivers' attitudes toward elder caregiving, we asked them to rate their level of agreement with three statements embodying typical perceptions of factors that might motivate people to undertake this task. Men in the national sample expressed greatest agreement with a statement suggesting that those engaged in elder caregiving experience considerable emotional gratification. In contrast, they tended to disagree with a statement that the prospect of collecting inheri-

tance is a motivating factor in elder caregiving; and virtually
none of the local sample mentioned collecting inheritance as an
incentive to caregiving. Several men in the local Delaware Valley
sample referred to caregiving as a "labor of love." One man said
it "makes me happy" to take care of his 96-year-old mother.
Another, caring for his wife of 60 years, said, simply, "I enjoy
it." National respondents agreed least with a statement that elder
caregiving provides a good opportunity to reduce longstanding
guilt feelings.

The level of agreement with the statement related to experiencing emotional gratification from elder caregiving was higher
to a statistically significant degree than that for both the statement about collecting inheritance and the one related to reduction of guilt feelings. Although the national sample minimized
guilt as a motivator in caregiving, narrative responses by men in
the local sample suggest that, for many of them, guilt reduction
was an issue. Asked to consider how he would feel if he were
not providing care, one man acting as the primary caregiver for
both his parents said, "It would be like abandoning my folks.
The only way I'd stop is if something physically happened to
me." Another man, caring for his great aunt, declared, "I'd
never forgive myself if something happened to her . . . . I just
wouldn't stop doing it. She'd be unhappy and I would have a
broken heart." Overall, however, local caregivers, like those in
Motenko's (1988) small sample, appeared to be motivated primarily by feelings of love and commitment that transcended
other potential incentives.

Male Caregivers' Attitudes toward the Elderly

To a series of statements reflecting stereotypic attitudes toward
the elderly, these male caregivers' responses indicated relative
neutrality. The statement toward which they expressed most
agreement was a positive one that older people do not spend
excessive time prying into others' affairs. They also leaned toward some agreement with a statement that older people are apt
to complain. Lowest levels of agreement were found for state-

ments that older people are set in their ways and resist change and that they are often against societal reform and want to hang on to the past. These men, in other words, did not appear to have strong stereotypic biases toward the elderly; but neither did they discount them entirely.

Male Caregivers' Instrumental and Affective Personality Traits

As explicated in chapter two, elder caregiving—indeed caregiving in general—has been provided by women in this culture and, thus, has been associated with nurturant, expressive personality attributes typically associated with the female sex role. Men's traditional sex role socialization has confined them to providing care from the emotional periphery of the family where they engage in instrumental tasks associated with providing and protecting. But recent research suggests that, in the wake of the women's movement, contemporary men find increasing cultural permission to be nurturant and affective—and to express these attributes through caring for others. Of particular relevance to elder caregiving are findings that suggest that as men reach middle and late life, they naturally become more nurturant (Gutmann 1987; Lowenthal, Thurnher & Chiriboda 1977). To assess how men in this study viewed themselves along the instrumental-to-affective continuum, we asked them to rate the extent to which they would describe themselves according to ten adjectives (on a scale from "rarely or never" to "almost always"). Five of these adjectives—"self-sufficient," "analytical," "competitive," "aggressive," and "forceful"—have traditionally been associated with the male sex role. The other five—"gentle," "compassionate," "warm," "loving," and "yielding"—have been associated with the female sex role (Bem 1974). Taken together these items comprise a Sex Role Index, which represents a shortened version of a composite measure of gender orientation developed by Bem (1974). Factor analysis performed on the items in this index produced two factors—each containing four items. An instrumental role factor was composed of the items "aggressive," "an-

alytical," "forceful," and "competitive." The affective role factor
contained the items "loving," compassionate," "gentle," and
"warm." (See appendix A for a full explanation of the index and
factors.)

As seen in table 8–1, the summary index score on the Sex
Role Index suggests a considerable degree of androgyny in these
men's perceptions of themselves. They tended to describe themselves with both instrumental and affective adjectives. But a look
at the pattern of ratings for individual adjectives reveals that
these men saw themselves as more affective than instrumental. It
is true that the highest mean item score was obtained for "self-
sufficient," reflecting the societal press for men to be independent and take care of themselves. But the four adjectives

Table 8–1

*Extent to Which Male Caregivers Described Themselves According to
Adjectives Representing Instrumental or Affective Personality Traits
(Sex Role Index)[a]*

Adjectives	Mean	S.D.	Rank
Self-Sufficient	4.30	.81	1
Gentle	4.07	.86	2
Compassionate	3.99	.92	3
Warm	3.98	.89	4
Loving	3.89	.94	5
Analytical	3.52	1.17	6
Yielding	2.80	.97	7
Competitive	2.80	1.26	8
Aggressive	2.54	1.15	9
Forceful	2.53	1.04	10
Summary index score	3.44	.53	

Factors	Mean	S.D.	Rank	t-value I × II
I Affective	3.94	.76	1	11.06*
II Instrumental	2.89	.82	2	

[a]Score Range = 1–5, where 1 = rarely or never, 2 = sometimes, 3 = often,
4 = usually, and 5 = almost always.
*$p < .001$

receiving the next highest ratings were all affective adjectives; and the three receiving the lowest ratings were instrumental adjectives. In fact, as seen in the "Factors" section of the table, the mean score for the Affective factor was significantly higher than was that for the Instrumental factor. Overall, then, these male caregivers appeared to see themselves as possessing measurable degrees of the affective, expressive, and nurturing personality traits usually associated with the female sex role.

Sex Role Index scores did not vary to a statistically significant degree in relation to the caregivers' marital status, their employment status, their overall physical health or whether they were caring for a spouse or another relative. The fact that no statistically significant difference emerged in relation to the caregivers' age challenges previous research suggesting that men may become more androgynous as they get older (Gutmann 1987; Neugarten 1968). The lack of difference may be due, however, to the fact that the variable "Age" was divided for purposes of analysis into age ranges that did not sufficiently differentiate younger male caregivers from those who were middle aged or older. And, of course, our data were based on a cross-sectional analysis rather than a longitudinal one.

Whatever their self-perceptions, responses by local Delaware Valley caregivers tended to reflect traditional stereotypic conceptions of gender roles and attributes. Asked about differences in the ways men and women give care, for example, one man caring for his wife declared that "women are more sensitive and in some ways more knowledgable [about caregiving]. They relate better . . . . Men are more brutal [and] try to put things out of their minds." Another believed that male caregivers are "more efficient and less tender." Another thought that "women in general have a more loving approach. Men are more likely to be matter-of-fact." One man caring for his 91-year-old mother suggested that "men tend to want to be macho and that doesn't seem to be compatible with nurturing." Repeatedly, terms like tender, patient, intuitive, and compassionate appeared as men talked about female caregivers, while they characterized men as efficient, tough-minded, or even insensitive.

Several explicitly ascribed such gender differences to sex role socialization. For example, one man thought differences were "due to socialization, to [women's experience] dealing with female issues." Another thought he was limited in caregiving because "I don't have the background in our sexist society." Another commented, "Men don't regard [caregiving] as their role in life. If there is a woman around, she is the one who has to do it." The same respondent went on to cite women's experience in caring for children as a determinant, as did a number of others. As one gentleman put it, experience with child care gives women "the mothering touch" with elderly relatives.

Other local caregivers, in contrast, thought that differences derived more from personality and temperament than from socialization and experience. One man caring for his 88-year-old mother, for example, thought that comfort with caregiving is "a personal concern. It depends on temperament—the concerns and qualities of a person—not on gender differences. Women have had more experience, but men can be as good at caretaking as women."

This opinion was mirrored in the perceptions of several of the female care recipients in the local sample. To most of those able to be interviewed, the fact that their caregivers were male made no apparent difference. As one 80-year-old woman whose disabilities necessitated high levels of personal care commented, "anybody who can help is what I need. Gender is not a factor." · Another thought that men were physically stronger—"but after that, there is no difference once they know what to do."

One woman with a degenerative disease provided an account of her caregiving encounters with both men and women that revealed some of the subtle nuances of the relational aspects of gender differences:

> "At first men perceive me as disabled and then change—more so than women. Women approach me more quickly and ask what they can do. They will sustain eye contact and will not be put off by how I appear. Women are more condescending, however. They will "baby down" to me in conversation.

It is, of course, impossible to generalize from such anecdotal responses to all male caregivers. What does emerge from local respondents' narrative accounts is a sense that, in spite of having internalized prevailing sex role stereotypes, these men provide care that reflects a degree of integration of affective and instrumental dimensions.

Correlations between Sex Role Index Factors and Other Study Variables

To explore possible relationships between instrumental and affective personality traits and previously discussed study variables, Pearson's correlations were examined between these two Sex Role Index factors, four key caregiving relationship indices, three task-related indices, and the Barriers to Caregiving index. The affective personality trait factor was not correlated to a statistically significant degree with the instrumental trait factor, suggesting that, indeed, they were measuring distinctly different personality dimensions.

As seen in table 8–2, there was a weak but statistically significant association between higher affective self-ratings and lower levels of reported caregiving burden. In contrast, the corre-

Table 8–2
Pearson's Correlations Between Instrumental and Affective Personality Trait Ratings and Other Study Variables

	Affective traits	Instrumental traits
Burden Index	−.15*	−.05
Recipient Affection Index	.10	.05
Provider Affection Index	.41***	.24**
Quality of Relationship Index	.15	.07
Task Frequency Index	.12	.13
Task Competence Index	.22*	.21*
Task Satisfaction Index	.17	.44**
Barriers to Caregiving Index	−.09	.18*

*p ≤.05

**p ≤.01

***p ≤.001

lation between the instrumental ratings and level of burden was negligible. In light of previously reported research suggesting that female caregivers experience more burden than do their male counterparts (Barusch & Spaid 1989; George 1984; Young & Kahana 1989), this finding appears anomalous. It may be, however, that mid-life men who are finding in caregiving an opportunity to express affective dimensions of themselves experience less burden than those who define themselves in traditional, instrumental terms. The weakness of the correlation, however, makes this conclusion tentative at best.

Affective personality traits were strongly related to the degree of affection expressed by the caregivers. In other words, those caregivers describing themselves in terms of affective attributes tended to rate themselves as more frequently listening to what the recipients said, displaying physical affection, expressing concern and sympathy, and inquiring about the recipients' well-being. Those caregivers rating themselves higher on affective traits also reported greater degrees of affiliativeness and intimacy between themselves and the recipients of their care, an association that did not hold true for those describing themselves in instrumental terms. Here, as might be expected, an affective self-definition appeared to be congruent with a capacity for higher levels of affection and intimacy.

There were no statistically significant correlations between the two major sex role trait factors and the index that measured how frequently male caregivers performed a variety of caregiving tasks. An examination of the four factors comprising this index—instrumental, functional, case management, and social support task factors—was more revealing. Specifically, higher ratings on "instrumental" traits were associated with a greater frequency of performing case management tasks and social support tasks. It is expectable that those giving themselves more instrumental self-ratings saw themselves as more frequently arranging outside services, supervising other caregiver assistants, and engaging in other aspects of case management. This finding lends support to Pruchno and Resch's (1989) conclusion that taking care of the management of caregiving is in line with typically masculine, instrumental proclivities that men have learned to exercise in roles of authority at home and in the workplace. The association between higher instrumental self-ratings and social support tasks is more surprising, but in line with previously reported findings about men's comfort with these tasks. Apparently the men providing high levels of companionship, emotional sustenance, and other dimensions of social support to their care recipients did not necessarily describe themselves in affective terms (the correlation here was negligible), but rather found these activities to be compatible with an instrumental self-definition. In other words, these men appeared comfortable with a degree of androgyny. Like the men described by Gutmann (1987), they may have seen themselves as possessing many cross-sex-typed assets but did not view themselves as any less masculine.

Overall, task competence was related to a statistically significant degree to both affective self-ratings and instrumental self-ratings. In individual factor scores statistically significant correlations appeared between affective ratings and level of competence in performing personal care tasks, case management tasks, and social support tasks—but not between these ratings and competence in performing instrumental tasks of daily living. In terms of caregiving competence, then, more traditional gender self-definitions appear to prevail. This finding is mirrored in associations between task factor scores and instrumental self-descriptions. The strongest correlation was found here with instrumental tasks, followed by case management tasks and social support tasks, with only a negligible correlation with personal care tasks. The similarity in correlations between both gender trait factors and the social support factor suggests that androgyny, more than a primarily instrumental or affective self-description, is associated with competence in performing social support tasks. One man in the local sample who was caring for his sister spoke to social shifts and increasing androgyny in caregiving: "It's changing: now men and women . . . do the same things."

The level of reported satisfaction in performing caregiving tasks was not correlated to a statistically significant degree to the affective personality trait ratings. Surprisingly, there was a

moderately strong correlation between satisfaction and instrumental self-ratings. Positive and statistically significant associations appeared between these ratings and the functional, case
management, and social support task factors. The correlation
between the instrumental self-ratings and the level of satisfaction in performing instrumental tasks of daily living approached but did not reach statistical significance. Apparently,
then, those male caregivers defining themselves in primarily
instrumental terms did not necessarily live out the prevailing
stereotype that they would find more satisfaction helping with
instrumental tasks while disliking the hands-on aspects of personal care.

Overall, the more the male caregivers described themselves
in instrumental terms, the more likely they were to experience
a variety of barriers to carrying out their caregiving tasks.
Scores on the Barriers to Caregiving Index were not correlated
to a statistically significant degree with affective self-ratings,
but were associated with instrumental self-ratings; that is, the
more instrumental the self-description, the greater the extent to
which barriers interfered with caregiving. Again, a look at individual factors was illuminating. Those male caregivers giving
themselves higher ratings on affective traits reported being less
impeded in their caregiving by barriers associated with physical
and emotional health factors. Just the opposite was true for
those defining themselves in more instrumental terms; here, a
more instrumental self-definition was associated, though not to
a statistically significant degree, with increased levels of impediment from physical and emotional health barriers. Similarly,
those describing themselves according to instrumental adjectives
experienced more barriers related to community and family
support and to gender-related factors, such as their own and
others' opinions of appropriate male behavior. Perhaps those
who saw themselves as more affective in nature found it easier
to express the dependency inherent in asking for community
and family support and were less concerned about "appropriate" gender roles than were men who saw themselves as primarily instrumental.

Summary

The male caregivers in this sample appeared to approach their tasks with an attitude that elder caregiving can bring considerable emotional gratification. Their responses did not suggest that they believe people provide such care in hopes of collecting inheritance or in order to reduce guilt feelings. To the extent that their attitudes expressed aspects of their own motivations, their engagement in caregiving was based in caring and altruism.

Similarly, these caregivers' responses to a number of statements embodying stereotypes toward elderly people suggested that they did not view their elders as nosy, complaining, set in their ways, or opposed to needed reform. Perhaps their experience on the front lines of caregiving has helped diminish such stereotypes.

Finally, men in this sample tended to define themselves in terms that reflected considerable androgyny. In fact, they described themselves in affective terms to a greater degree than instrumental terms. Comments by men in the local sample, however, suggested that, whatever their self-perceptions, they had internalized traditional stereotypic conceptions of gender characteristics. An affective self-definition was associated with lower levels of caregiving burden, higher frequency of initiating affection with care recipients, increased levels of affiliativeness and affection with recipients, and a greater sense of competence in caregiving—but not with the level of satisfaction in this task. An instrumental self-definition, although not correlated with burden, was associated with the degree to which caregivers reported various barriers to caregiving. Higher ratings on instrumental adjectives by these caregivers were also correlated with their initiating more affectionate behavior with their recipients, and with higher levels of both reported competence and satisfaction in caregiving.

These findings present a mixed picture of male caregivers' gender-related attitudes that is more suggestive than conclusive. Nevertheless, the degree of androgyny reflected in our findings suggests that those planning policies, programs, and services for male elder caregivers should not restrict themselves to traditional conceptions of the male gender role. Rather, planners should be guided by a flexible view of mid- and late life that takes men's nurturant, expressive strivings into consideration. Such a view makes it possible to help men benefit from elder caregiving as a potentially gratifying developmental opportunity.

9
Do Caregiver Support Groups Really Help?

In previous chapters of this book we have documented that the male caregivers in the national and local samples were performing a wide range of tasks. Their sense of competence, feelings of satisfaction, aspects of burden, and various barriers they experienced in carrying out these tasks were examined. We have presented data that describe the formal and informal supports caregivers used and explored the family context of their caregiving, including affective and attitudinal components of the men's relationships with their care recipients.

We now turn to a report of how the men in this study made use of caregiver support groups. How did the structure and function of these groups address their special needs? What was it like for them to participate in support groups comprised mostly of women? How was support group attendance associated with the variables described above? Answers to these questions derive from both the survey of the male caregivers themselves and from leaders and organizers of the support groups they attended.

The Structure and Function of Caregiver Support Groups

Before examining gender-related dimensions of caregiver support groups specifically, it is important to identify the structure and function of the groups in which men participated. A section of the questionnaire distributed to leaders and organizers addressed the mechanics of the groups they led. As seen in table 9–1, most (62 percent) of the groups met monthly; only 20 percent met biweekly, and even fewer (12 percent) met weekly. Meetings were held at a consistent location, usually a facility for the aged (37 percent) or a public building (24 percent), on the same day and at the same time. Half the leaders reported that their meetings lasted between one and two hours; another 37 percent said meetings lasted two hours. Over 80 percent reported that they followed an established format in conducting the meetings. Personal sharing, information exchange, mutual support, and problem solving were salient components of the average group session. Many groups occasionally used guest speakers.

These appeared to be well-established groups, 60 percent of them having met for more than three years; their composition was stable. Ninety percent were ongoing rather than time-limited

Table 9–1
*Structural and Functional Characteristics
of Caregiver Support Groups*

	Number	*Percentage*
Frequency of group meetings		
More than once a week	0	0.0
Once a week	18	12.3
Once every two weeks	31	21.2
Once every month	90	61.6
Less than once per month	7	4.8
Total	146	100.0
Consistent meeting location		
Yes	143	97.3
No	4	2.7
Total	147	100.0
Location of group meetings		
Someone's home	4	2.7
A church/synagogue	26	17.6
A facility for the aged	54	36.5
A public building	35	23.6
A community agency	29	19.6
Total	148	100.0

Table 9–1 continued

	Number	Percentage
Length of the average meeting		
One hour or less	7	4.7
Between one and two hours	76	51.4
Two hours	54	36.5
More than two hours	11	7.4
Total	148	100.0
Tenure of the group		
Less than 6 months	15	10.4
Between 6 and 12 months	13	9.0
Between 1 and 2 years	13	9.0
Between 2 and 3 years	17	11.8
Between 3 and 5 years	43	29.9
More than 5 years	43	29.9
Total	144	100.0
Composition of the group		
Very stable	43	29.7
Somewhat stable	84	57.9
Somewhat unstable	17	11.7
Very unstable	1	.7
Total	145	100.0
Consistent meeting day/time		
Yes	136	93.2
No	10	6.8
Total	146	100.0
Single- or team-led groups		
Single	74	52.1
Team	68	47.9
Total	142	100.0
Group permanency		
Limited	15	10.1
Ongoing	133	89.9
Total	148	100.0
Cost of operating groups		
No cost	48	38.4
Some cost	77	61.6
Total	125	100.0

groups. Roughly half were led by a single leader, while the other half were led by a team. Most organizers reported that there was some cost to operating their groups. Although 32 percent received private donations, and a quarter got help from businesses or corporations, very few were funded from government grants, foundation grants, or church or civic groups. Only one in ten charged dues to their members.

Most leaders reported that they depended on word of mouth as a means of attracting potential group members. The next most popular recruiting methods were newspaper advertisements, posters or flyers, and informational speeches at senior centers or community forums. Only a third used radio and television ads. Less than 10 percent relied on newsletters or information and referral sources as recruiting devices.

Gender-Related Characteristics of Support Groups

To begin to identify areas in which the support groups addressed the needs of men specifically, we asked group leaders to respond to questions about efforts to reach out to male caregivers, factors affecting men's participation, and possible factors deterring men from joining. As seen in table 9–2, most of the groups (95 percent) did not make special efforts to advertise their activities to male caregivers. Nevertheless, men did reach the groups; nearly 90 percent of the groups responding to our survey said they were composed of both men and women. On the average, however, there were twice as many women as men in these groups, and nearly a third of the leaders thought that men's attendance was less regular than women's. Similarly, more women than men served as leaders in team-led groups.

Three-quarters of the leaders reported that the functioning of their support groups was not affected by the group's gender makeup. Similarly, nearly 70 percent believed that discussion was evenly distributed between the sexes. Those citing one sex as dominant, however, cited women much more frequently than men. Nearly 70 percent reported that the men in their groups did not appear to be seeking to have needs met that were unique to their gender.

Table 9–2
Gender-Related Characteristics of Caregiver Support Groups

	Number	Percentage
Special efforts to advertise the groups to male caregivers		
Yes	7	4.8
No	139	95.2
Total	146	100.0
Gender composition of the groups		
Mixed	132	89.8
Single sexed, female	12	8.2
Single sexed, male	3	2.0
Total	147	100.0
Current participation in mixed groups		
Men	5.16 (mean)	
Women	11.96 (mean)	
Men's attendance patterns compared to womens' patterns		
Less regular	38	29.0
As regular	82	62.6
More regular	11	8.4
Total	131	100.0
Proportion of male/female leaders in team-led groups		
Male	.38 (mean)	
Female	1.84 (mean)	
Functioning of groups affected by sexual makeup		
Yes	36	26.9
No	98	73.1
Total	134	100.0
Does one sex dominate group discussion		
No, it is evenly distributed	88	67.7
Yes, the women dominate	36	27.7
Yes, the men dominate	6	4.6
Total	130	100.0
Unique needs for men in groups		
Yes	41	30.8
No	92	69.2
Total	133	100.0

(Mean) = average number of men or women in each group.

When asked what they thought deterred men from joining caregiver support groups, the leaders most frequently mentioned the traditional attitude that men should be able to handle caregiving without assistance. Many believed that, for men, attending a support group constituted an admission of weakness, loss of control, and, ultimately failure. As one put it, "men are deterred by the word 'support.' Most men did not attend the group until they felt like everything else had failed and they were failures." Another said that men are deterred because of the "macho feeling that they should be 'strong' and carry the burden alone. They are embarrassed to ask for help or even to accept it when offered."

Next most frequently mentioned was the belief that men have either an inability to engage in or a resistance to personal sharing. Most ascribed this reluctance to internalized societal attitudes that men should not "go public" with their problems. One group leader thought that "men have a tendency to keep their problems private and therefore do not readily seek help." Another suggested that men he had worked with experienced "fears of excessive self-disclosure and difficulty with communication of feelings."

Least frequently mentioned were health problems, lack of awareness of the group's existence, and misunderstandings about the group's purpose and function such as viewing the group as exclusively "touchy-feely." As support group leaders viewed it, therefore, factors related to traditional sex role socialization appeared to be pivotal deterring influences. Once joining support groups, however, men tended to remain members as long as women. In fact, a slightly larger proportion of men than women had been in the support groups we surveyed for more than two years.

Men's Experience in Caregiver Support Groups

What were the views of male caregivers concerning their experience in caregiver support groups? To answer this question, we analyzed men's responses to a series of questions about their participation.

About a third of them reported that they had been attending support groups for less than a year; almost half had been attending between one and four years, and only a fifth had attended more than four years. Most (84 percent) of them had not been in caregiver support groups previously. Most reported their frequency of attendance as "almost always" (64 percent) or "very often" (23 percent).

Three-quarters of the men reported feeling "very comfortable" in sharing their experiences, and nearly another 20 percent felt "somewhat comfortable." Only just over 6 percent reported feeling uncomfortable. This contrasts with the perception of support group leaders who believed that many men had trouble with personal sharing. Sixty percent of the male caregivers believed they were just as active as women in these groups. Although a quarter thought they were more active than other men, only 8 percent thought they were more active than the women in their groups. As one of the caregivers in the local Delaware Valley sample put it, "I'm less able to talk in front of women."

More than three-quarters of the men reported being "very satisfied" with what they were getting from their caregiver support groups, and another 20 percent were "somewhat satisfied." This satisfaction may have translated into lower levels of stress for them. Nearly 50 percent believed that their caregiving had become "somewhat less stressful" since starting to attend a support group, and more than a quarter reported that caregiving was "much less stressful." Referring to the stress of caring for his elderly wife, one man in the local sample said, "If not for [the] group, I couldn't have done it. It prepares me to cope with things before I confront them. And it shows me that things could be worse."

Table 9–3 displays Pearson's correlations among the seven support group experience variables. Interestingly, the duration of membership in a group was not associated with level of comfort in sharing experience, activity levels, satisfaction with the group, nor with stress levels experienced in caregiving. The frequency of attendance, in contrast, was positively correlated with the level of comfort in sharing experiences. Men who attended more frequently also perceived themselves as more active than other men and more active than women in their groups. Lowered levels of

Table 9–3
Pearson's Correlations between Selected Support Group
Experience Variables

Support group experience variables	I	II	III	IV	V	VI	VII
I Duration of group membership	—						
II Frequency of attendance	−.03	—					
III Level of comfort in sharing experiences	.02	.34**	—				
IV Activity levels compared to other men	.20	.32**	.33**	—			
V Activity levels compared to women	.02	.31**	.37**	.28**	—		
VI Satisfaction with support group	.07	.10	.19*	.04	.11	—	
VII Level of stress since beginning group	−.13	−.19*	−.07	−.09	.01	−.31**	—

*p < .01
**p < .001

stress were also related to more frequent support group attendance.

Not surprisingly, the more comfortable men felt in sharing their caregiving experiences, the more active they were in comparison to other men and women. Comfort in sharing was also correlated with increased satisfaction with the group experience. When men reported that they were more active than other men in their groups, they also reported being more active than women. This suggests that general style of participation overrode gender factors as a correlate of relative activity. Finally, the more satisfied they were with their support group experience, the lower the levels of stress these men reported. Frequency of and satisfaction with support group attendance, therefore, appeared to have been more helpful than levels of participation in the group in understanding caregiver stress.

Neither duration of membership, frequency of attendance, level of comfort in sharing experiences, activity levels relative to other men and to women, satisfaction with their support groups, nor stress levels were related to whether or not the caregivers were caring for a spouse. Neither did scores on these support group experience variables differ to a statistically significant degree in association with the gender of the recipient, whether or not the caregiver considered himself to have primary caregiving responsibility, or whether or not the recipient was receiving community services. These aspects of support group experience did not differ significantly in relation to a number of caregiver variables including marital status, employment status, occupation, or whether or not the caregivers lived with the recipients of their care. Those men caring for recipients who had Alzheimer's disease reported longer periods of support group attendance then those caring for persons who did not have this illness. But whether or not the recipient had Alzheimer's was not associated with differences in scores for any of the other support group experience variables.

Interestingly, the older the recipient of their care the more comfortable male caregivers were in sharing their experiences in support groups. Also, the older the recipient, the more satisfied the men were with their support group experience. In addition, the older the caregivers were the more often they attended support groups, the more active they were in relation to other men, and the more satisfied they were with their group experiences. These findings suggest that the support groups may have been particularly facilitative contexts for older caregivers who were dealing with the most elderly recipients.

How did these seven support group experience variables relate to other aspects of caregiving? To answer this question, key health indices, task experience indices, relationship indices, and gender indices were correlated with the support group variables. Duration of support group membership was strongly correlated with the Activities of Daily Living Index, confirming that the more their recipients required help with these activities the longer male caregivers had been attending support groups. Similarly, duration of attendance correlated with the frequency with which the men performed caregiving tasks. The longer they had been attending support groups, the less the caregivers perceived their care recipients to initiate affectionate behavior with them

and the less satisfied they felt with the concern for them expressed by their recipients. Clearly, those attending support
groups longest were engaged in the care of recipients whose
long-term conditions were both demanding and draining.

Interestingly, the longer the men attended support groups,
the more competent they felt, especially in providing personal
care. Lower levels of reported competence in this area were
associated with more frequent group attendance, suggesting that
the men may have turned to the groups for help in developing
competence with such tasks as bathing, grooming, and toileting.
The frequency of attendance was also related to the way the men
viewed themselves in terms of gender attributes. Specifically,
those attending most frequently tended to describe themselves
less often in male-oriented instrumental terms such as self-
sufficient, analytical, forceful, and competitive. It is impossible to
determine whether seeing themselves as less instrumental resulted
from the men's more frequent attendance at support groups or
whether those describing themselves in this way were more likely
to be frequent attendees.

There was a moderate negative correlation between the level
of comfort the men felt in sharing their experiences and the
barriers they experienced in caregiving. This association was particularly striking in the case of physical and emotional health
barriers. Perhaps those men who believed that they were confronting relatively few barriers of this type were more comfortable sharing themselves in support groups. But it is also possible
that the ability to discuss these physical and interpersonal aspects
of caregiving made dealing with them easier.

Those caregivers reporting that they were more active than
the other men in their support groups reported higher levels of
competence in caregiving, particularly competence in performing
the instrumental tasks of daily living. Those viewing themselves
as more active than other men also reported more frequently
initiating affectionate behavior with their care recipients. Those
reporting that they were more active than the women in their
support groups reported experiencing less burden in caregiving.
Perhaps men's active involvement and ventilation in support
groups helped reduce their burden in caregiving. But, again, it

may be that those feeling the least burden were more comfortable sharing their experiences than those who felt more burden and were reluctant to reveal their vulnerability.

There was a positive correlation between the level of satisfaction the men experienced in their support groups and a higher incidence of health problems in their care recipients. This suggests the possibility that the groups may have been effective in addressing male caregivers' concerns about dealing with their recipients' health.

Not surprisingly, lower levels of stress were correlated to a statistically significant degree with higher levels of reported life satisfaction among these men and with greater frequency in the extent to which their recipients initiated affectionate behavior. Interpersonal and affective variables, therefore, seemed more related to stress levels than were factors like frequency, competence, and satisfaction in performing caregiving tasks, health factors, or gender-related issues. As Barnett and Baruch (1987) suggest, role quality appears to be a more significant correlate of stress and well-being than is role occupancy and its associated tasks.

Male Caregivers' Assessment of Caregiver Support Groups

Both the survey administered to the national sample and the questionnaire administered to the local sample gave caregivers an opportunity to cite the best and worst things about the support groups they attended. As indicated in table 9–4, in connection with the best aspects of their groups, the factor mentioned most frequently was the opportunity to be with people who were having similar experiences and feelings. The following comments were typical:

> Members have an opportunity to discuss their problems with each other so they do not feel alone.

> [The support group offers the] opportunity to share needs and feelings with those "who have been there."

Table 9–4

*Male Caregiver Views of the Best and Worst Things
About Caregiver Support Groups*

	Number	Percentage	Rank
Best things about support groups			
You are with people who have similar experiences/feelings	97	32.1	1
You get support from others	67	22.4	2
Problems are resolved	39	13.0	3
It provides information about community supports	36	12.1	4
You learn the skills of caregiving	17	5.7	5
You learn how to deal with guilt/anger/depression	15	5.0	6
It is a chance to help others	12	4.0	7
It is a break/respite	11	3.7	8
You learn about what to expect in the future	6	2.0	9
Total	300	100.0	
Worst things about support groups			
It is depressing/demoralizing	21	35.6	1
Certain members dominate the discussion	15	25.4	2
It is a reminder that impairment is irreversible	8	13.6	3
Information is irrelevant/not helpful	7	11.8	4
You learn what to expect for the future	4	6.8	5
The same people attend each meeting	2	3.4	6
It doesn't provide diversion from my problems	2	3.4	6
Total	59	100.0	

Support group participants from the local Delaware Valley echoed this emphasis. One reported benefiting most from "finding out I wasn't the only one." Another appreciated "knowing you were in good company."

Next most frequently cited as best was the opportunity to receive emotional support from others. One man, for example, liked his group because he received "support from others with [the] same problems." Another gentleman reported that members of his support group had been able to "make lasting friends and become a 'family'." That more than half the national sample cited personal sharing and the opportunity for emotional support as most beneficial is somewhat surprising in light of previous research suggesting that male participants prefer concrete, practical information over discussion of affective issues. The next most frequently mentioned positive aspects of support group attendance were the opportunity for problem resolution, the opportunity to learn information about community supports, and the chance to learn caregiving skills. As one man put it, the support group "offers a way to learn useful information regarding actual daily, real problems, as well as related topics such as legal problems, medical needs, and how to get help." Only a handful of men saw group attendance as respite from their tasks or as a chance to learn about what to expect in the future.

Asked to describe the worst aspects of attending support groups, the most frequently mentioned concern was that they were depressing or demoralizing. Typical was the comment, "It is depressing learning other people's troubles." Another man mentioned being depressed by listening to "One woman with more problems than the world could solve; I didn't go because of her." In light of research suggesting that caregivers of both genders cope with their situations in part by minimizing the gravity of their problems and screening out negative feelings (Winogrand et al. 1987), it may be that these men's coping strategies were threatened by such negative content. Since it is unlikely that support groups of this type could avoid such content, leaders should be attentive to men's reactions and help them express their feelings.

Next most frequently mentioned as a negative aspect of support group attendance was that certain group members tended to dominate discussion. One man reported that the worst aspect of his support group was "Those that [sic] monopolize all the support group time with their own problems." Another was troubled by "Individuals who want to hold the floor too long, though the chairperson makes attempts to shorten the speech." Complaints suggest that group leaders need to arm themselves with skills that help them ensure balanced participation.

Next in frequency were comments that group attendance reminded them that their recipients' impairments were irreversible. One man reported that "hearing about no progress in a cure" was discouraging. Another found it difficult "knowing that we are all fighting a losing battle with no possible help for the patient." For one of the local caregivers, group attendance was negative because, "It makes me realize that my wife is now coming to the worst stage of her illness." Although a few men thought that they didn't receive useful information and that group attendance offered them no diversion from their problems, it appeared to be the factors related to confronting painful feelings and dealing with unwieldy group members that were least satisfying.

Recommendations for Improving Caregiver Support Groups

Both support group leaders and the male caregivers responded to questions about how the groups could be improved in order to be more responsive to the needs of men who attend them. Specifically, the leaders made recommendations about how to encourage greater participation by male caregivers in their groups. The most frequent suggestions spoke to the need for increased publicity, particularly publicity that emphasizes attention to men's caregiving concerns. Recommendations included contacting men's fraternal organizations, putting men's pictures in fliers advertising support groups, and publicizing the groups at health clubs. The leaders also suggested that male group members be encouraged to let other men in their situation know about the groups. For example, one leader encouraged organizing a "bring-a-male-friend" meeting. Another thought that providing male group participants with names and phone numbers of potential male attendees would enhance recruitment. Others suggested a "men's night." In conjunction with such concrete suggestions, many leaders emphasized the importance of letting potential male participants know that other men attend support groups and that they are not alone.

A question in the instrument administered to the national sample of male caregivers asked them to suggest ways in which support groups could be more helpful to them and other men. The most frequent suggestion was that more relevant information be provided. One caregiver was specific: "Place emphasis on trying to obtain the most qualified speakers in medicine, legal considerations, pharmacy, community support, and patient needs." Another recommended detailed information on "caregiving skills."

The previously reported finding of a negative correlation between frequency of support group attendance and perceived caregiving competence suggests the possibility that these men may have turned to the groups for assistance in increasing their competence. To the extent that information can be assumed to enhance competence, it is not surprising that men wanted more.

A smaller proportion suggested more frequent meetings might be helpful. Since they appeared to see the social support aspects of group attendance as the most useful dimension, it is not surprising that they would suggest more frequent opportunities to make and sustain connections with other group members. This possibility was reflected by one man who suggested increasing the frequency of meetings so that members could "really know each other. Part of our time, of necessity, is taken by speakers teaching on valuable subjects, but it limits 'sharing' time."

Summary

The findings reported above suggest that the male caregivers in the national sample had access to meetings of regularly scheduled, ongoing support groups that were stable in composition and provided opportunities for personal sharing, social support, and access to information. Although the group leaders we surveyed reported that most groups contained both men and women, very few appeared to make special efforts to reach out specifically to potential male participants. Women outnumbered men by far in most mixed gender groups. The leaders' perception was that among the most salient factors deterring men from joining such groups were traditional male attitudes that men should be able to handle caregiving without support and that they were resistant to personal sharing. Those men who did attend, however, did so as regularly as the women in their groups and had been attending as long as women.

Those male caregivers attending support groups reported

feeling comfortable, believed themselves to be as active as other men and women in their groups, and were satisfied overall with what they were receiving from the groups. The majority thought that the stress they experienced in caregiving had been reduced since beginning to attend.

Aspects of the male caregivers' experience of support group attendance appeared to be related to a variety of other aspects of the overall caregiving experience, particularly the frequency, competence, and satisfaction with which they reported performing caregiving tasks. These men reported that the opportunity to be with others sharing similar situations, support from others, and availability of competence-enhancing information were among the best aspects of group participation. As they viewed it, the depression they experienced hearing about others' problems and the dominance of the group by controlling group members constituted the worst aspects. Their recommendations for making the groups more helpful to men emphasized providing information that would facilitate their caregiving tasks and increasing the frequency of group meetings. Other suggestions for enhancing men's support group participation can be found in appendix B, "Practical Recommendations for Involving Men in Caregiver Support Groups."

10
Current Challenges, Future Directions

This book reports results from an inquiry into the lives of men providing care for an elderly relative. It draws upon the experiences of a group of dedicated individuals who have committed substantial portions of time and energy to a labor of love traditionally delegated to women. Having painted a portrait of the male elder caregiver—his tasks, barriers, burdens, gratifications, relationships, attitudes, and sources of support—what can we conclude about the services, programs, policies, and future research strategies that are most likely to meet his needs?

Some Implications for Practice and Policy

First, it is clear that there is an identifiable group of husbands, sons, grandsons, brothers, and other men who are deeply involved in providing primary care for an elderly relative, usually a woman. The caregiving commitments of the men in this sample, most of whom had reached late-middle or early old age themselves, required large measures of physical and emotional energy over the long haul. Most were caring for relatives who were impaired by the physical, mental, emotional, and behavioral sequelae of Alzheimer's disease or a related form of dementia. The apparent high incidence of Alzheimer's in this sample adds credence to recent research suggesting that this disease may be twice as common as was previously thought, afflicting as many of ten percent of those over age 65 and half of those over 85 (Purvis

1989). Since more women than men develop Alzheimer's (Fitting et al. 1986), men, especially husbands, emerge as likely candidates for providing the high levels of care they require. Those planning services and programs for male caregivers, therefore, need to address their needs for education about the nature and progression of Alzheimer's and for the hands-on skills required in giving what may become total care.

The majority of the men in our study were providing primary care with only uneven levels of family assistance; and, aside from their participation in the caregiver support groups from which the sample was drawn, most were not making use of formal support services. There was some evidence that, like men in other studies (Miller 1987; Motenko 1988), these respondents preferred to remain in control of the caregiving situation and wanted help with rather than relief from their duties. These findings further underscore the need for caregiving education and training programs that consider the male perspective. Increasingly, low-cost community-based programs help prepare new fathers for child care responsibilities. Perhaps the time has come for developing similarly designed programs that help prepare people to meet the unique demands of elder care.

Caregiving and the Workplace

For one in five of the men in this study, their capacity to "go it alone" as caregivers was compromised by full-time employment; another seven percent were working part time. Since most were not cutting back on hours at work to accommodate caregiving duties, we can assume that they, like Brody's (1981) "women in the middle," were juggling multiple and competing demands.

Fortunately, the workplace has begun to respond to the needs of people who must balance work and elder caregiving responsibilities. Increasingly, corporations offer caregiving information seminars as well as linkages for referral to formal support programs. Recently the American Association of Retired Persons developed a four-part "Caregivers in the Workplace" package, which can be adopted by both large and small businesses. The package's four components—a Caregiving Survey, Caregiving Fairs, an Educational Package, and a Care Management Guide—are designed to help participants manage the stresses of caregiving in ways that enable them to concentrate better at work. Included in the package are specific planning and training guides. Similarly, in Connecticut, the Corporate Elder-care Project at the University of Bridgeport's Center for the Study of Aging has set up a program at three corporations— Pitney Bowes, Remington, and People's Bank of Bridgeport—to establish a telephone helpline, worksite-based support groups, and lunchtime caregiving information exchanges for elder care-giving employees (Wood 1987).

Flexible work hours and elder care leave benefits are also offered by some corporations. These and similar initiatives seem especially relevant in light of recent research suggesting that tra-ditional employee assistance programs may not meet the unique needs of working caregivers (Scharlach & Boyd 1989). It may be, however, that widespread availability of such supports will become a reality only as more corporate executives confront the demands of elder care in their own lives (Wood 1987).

The Retired Caregiver

And what about caregivers who are unemployed, as were nearly three out of four men in this study? These primarily middle-class men reported that they were managing fairly well financially; but they can hardly be considered representative of all male care-givers, many of whom face major financial hardships. Those applying to programs like Medicare and Medicaid for assistance learn quickly that they "are not public health *programs*, but are public *payment* systems for private enterprise in the health field" (Older Women's League [OWL] 1982/1987, p. 10). Before mak-ing use of Medicaid, for example, elders must deplete their per-sonal resources to the level of virtual impoverishment. And, given the high cost of elder care, reaching this level does not take long. A recent study by the House Select Committee on Aging revealed that half of all married couples "spend down" to eligibility within six months (Weinstein 1989).

The states are beginning to provide some help. A recent study suggests that at least 35 of them permit payments of vary-ing levels to relatives who provide home care (Linsk, Keigher &

Osterbusch 1988). And in the last few years some states have introduced tax deductions or tax credits for family caregiving (Kane 1985). Given the persistent salience of the value of family care in our culture, policies that provide financial subsidies or supplements for home care emerge as a priority. For male caregivers who appear to resist using outside services, such assistance may be particularly pertinent. Such programs will be costly and slow to come, but recent Congressional Resolutions designating a "National Family Caregivers' Week" indicates a broadening public awareness of the plight of those providing home elder care (OWL 1982/1987).

Tasks

Those caregivers in our sample were engaged in tasks representing the complete caregiving continuum—from providing companionship to managing recipients' incontinence. Their designation of companionship and emotional support tasks as those performed most frequently and with most satisfaction challenges conventional wisdom that male caregivers emphasize instrumental help while keeping their emotional distance. Yet these men did not feel entirely competent in this intimate arena; feelings of most competence were instead associated with traditionally masculine instrumental tasks. Perhaps those professionals assisting male caregivers need to help them recognize that quiet listening, handholding, and other forms of "just being there" represent a major contribution to the well-being of the recipients of their care.

Bearing out traditional concepts of male caregiving, our respondents helped their recipients least with bathing, grooming, toileting, and other aspects of personal care. Not surprisingly, it was these tasks to which they believed they brought least competence and from which they derived least satisfaction. Anecdotal reports from both caregivers and care recipients in the local Delaware Valley sample suggest that, with training, men do very well with personal care and learn not to mind it as much. Again, this points to the need for skills development; home health care training may be as valuable as assistance from home health aides to male caregivers.

The finding that personal care was the most burdensome task for our respondents may have to do with internalized ideas of the appropriate gender role allocation of caregiving responsibilites. Although the men's overall perceptions of the appropriate division of caregiving labor reflected considerable androgyny, they believed that the provision of personal care was women's work—an opinion shared by several local care recipients. Only as more men engage in the basic care of infants and elders are such views likely to change.

The Invisible Work

Overall, however, these men reported relatively low levels of burden—and this in spite of their perceptions that they put out much more than they got back in caregiving. An encouraging supportive family attitude toward the job they were doing was associated with less burden and appeared to make more difference than actual concrete assistance from relatives. The seemingly paradoxical finding that feelings of burden *increased* in association with outside assistance is in line with some other research results. Miller (1987), for example, found that men displayed less stress and strain as they felt in charge of the caregiving situation. Once again, a sense of mastery and control appears to be crucial to the male caregiver's sense of well-being.

As described earlier, our respondents approached elder care with a belief that it could provide them with emotional gratification. They appeared to be motivated by an ethic of caring and altruism more than by a sense of guilt, duty, or greed. Neither negative stereotypic attitudes toward caregiving nor negative biases toward the elderly dominated their experience. And although their self-descriptions reflected androgyny, they tended to identify themselves in terms of affective, expressive traits usually associated with the female sex role. Whether these were men who had naturally become more feminized with middle age, became more affective through caregiving, or ended up as caregivers because of a proclivity toward communal, expressive personality traits is impossible to determine.

It is interesting, on the other hand, that those providing high levels of companionship, emotional closeness, and other aspects of social support tended to describe themselves more frequently in traditionally masculine, instrumental terms. What emerges here is a mixed picture. Perhaps these men had achieved considerable integration of affective and instrumental traits that transcended stereotypic conceptions of the kinds of care men and women "should" be providing.

Support Groups

A sense of integration appeared to characterize men's experiences in caregiver support groups. Contrary to what might be expected, those attending such groups were active, comfortable, and relatively open about their feelings. Opportunities for interpersonal sharing and social support were among the most attractive features of attendance for them. This finding appears to be at odds with perceptions of caregiver support group leaders who believed that men's preference for independence and resistance to personal sharing reduced their attendance relative to women. It seems more likely that men's lower attendance resulted from a lack of recruitment; only a handful of leaders reported reaching out to men specifically. That support group attendance was associated with less stress and was in other ways beneficial to our respondents suggests that creative outreach strategies could help men use an inexpensive source of support that could enhance their well-being considerably. Some specific ideas for supporting men's participation appear in appendix B.

Implications for Future Research

Given other research findings that suggest that men tend not to join caregiver support groups (Hlavaty 1986), the men in our study may have been unique. The selection effects secondary to drawing a sample from support groups limits the generalizability of our findings considerably. We have no way of knowing whether or not these respondents were typical of male caregivers who have not joined such groups.

Due to this and other threats to internal and external validity, many questions remain unanswered. For example, would those men who have not participated in support groups also report low levels of caregiving burden? Is there a large invisible cohort of male caregivers whose allegiance to the "stiff-upper-lip" stereotype of masculine coping styles keeps them from using support groups and other services? Our guess is that this is the case.

There is no question that women continue to predominate as caregivers of the elderly. According to a recent study by the American Association of Retired Persons and the Travelers Companies Foundation, three out of four of America's seven million elder caregivers are women (Weinstein 1989). The feminization of caregiving is deeply embedded in our culture and slow to change. As Brody (1986) points out, "The behavior of adult children tells us that women *and* men continue to accept the proposition that it is women's role to provide the day-to-day care of the old" (p. 198).

Yet at least a quarter of elder caregivers—as many as a third in some clinical settings (Zarit et al. 1986)—are men. This means that, at a minimum, there are 1,750,000 husbands, sons, grandsons, and other men taking care of a frail, elderly relative. And while the predicted increases in their ranks are unlikely to offset the increments in caregiving demands on women, their unique strengths, vulnerabilities, and coping styles merit further study.

As suggested earlier, random samples drawn from among all male caregivers would be more representative than the convenience sample of support group members chosen for this study. In addition, ours was a remarkably homogeneous sample, tapping a population of white, well-educated, middle-class, retired men. As Jackson (1989) and others suggest, studies that examine the elder care configurations of families who differ in race, ethnicity, and social class from this much-studied population are long overdue.

Studies that employ comparison groups not only minimize some of the selection effects operating in this study, but they help surface differences between subgroups of caregivers. Much could be learned about the unique experiences of male elder caregivers by comparing them to a group of men engaged in another form of caregiving—primary caretaking fathers, for example. In addition, our research suggests that frequently male elder caregiving stretches across many years as care recipients live into periods of extended chronic illness. Longitudinal studies, therefore, could help explicate the nature of shifts and transitions in men's caregiving over the long haul—a perspective that will become more and more meaningful as longevity increases.

Although this study attempted to include qualitative findings via interviews with a small subsample of caregivers and recipients, it remains primarily a descriptive and correlational inquiry. Future research that includes ethnographic methods designed to capture the intersubjective phenomonology of male caregiving would add a much needed in-depth perspective (Kaye & Applegate in press). Because the study of male elder caregiving is still in its infancy, strategies like those recommended by Rowles and Reinharz (1988), which integrate quantitative and qualitative methods more systematically, will be especially helpful. As families continue to change and learn to diversify and share their multiple roles and responsibilites in new ways, the challenge of charting the experiences of men engaged in caregiving across the life cycle will offer exciting research opportunities.

APPENDIX A
Scale and Index Construction

Appendix A contains definitions of the major study indices and factors and includes related statistics. This section should prove useful for those readers wishing more detail about the procedures and specific measures used in the analysis. Indices developed by others are highlighted in table A–1. Index item information and index and factor statistics are presented in tables A–2 and A–3. Statistical terminology is explained in a straight forward fashion in appendix C.

The Study Indices

A. Task Frequency Index. This index gauges the extent to which male caregivers perform various types of caregiving tasks. Task frequency measures both the frequency or repetitiveness of individual task performance as well as the level of multiple task performance. This 22-item index is scored on a 4-point scale in which 0 = never, 1 = rarely, 2 = sometimes, and 3 = often. The items included in the scale are:

1. Preparing meals

2. Marketing or shopping

3. Household cleaning

4. Laundry

5. Escort to the doctor's office

6. Companionship and emotional support

7. Help with dressing

8. Help with shaving, brushing hair, putting on makeup, applying ointments or lotions

9. Help with eating meals

10. Help with getting in and out of bed

11. Help with going to the bathroom

12. Help with bathing

13. Help with paying bills or writing checks

14. Help with taking medications or injections

15. Help with home repairs

16. Help with writing letters or filling out forms

17. Speaking on behalf of relative/friend at community agencies

18. Arranging for outside services

19. Supervising the help other friends/relatives provide

20. Supervising the help paid workers provide

21. Help with legal matters

22. Help with use of the telephone

The reliability coefficient was .93. The scale mean and standard deviation were 1.96 and .74 respectively.

B. Task Satisfaction Index. This index measures the extent of satisfaction felt by male caregivers in performing the identical series of caregiving tasks comprising the Task Frequency Index. This 22-item index is scored on a 4-point scale in which 0 = not satisfying at all, 1 = not very satisfying, 2 = somewhat satisfying, and 3 = extremely satisfying. The items included in the scale are listed above. The reliability coefficient was .95. The

Table A–1

Previously Developed Indices Utilized in the Male Caregiver (MCG) Survey Questionnaire

Content Area	Source	Version
Illness index	Shanas (1962)	Modified
ADL scale	Horowitz and Dobrof (1980)	Modified
Self-assessed health	CSAHD (1978)	Modified
Mental health	CSAHD (1978)	Modified
Overall mental health	CSAHD (1978)	Original
Living arrangements	Horowitz and Dobrof (1980)	Original
Ethnic origin	Stone, Cafferata, and Sangl (1987)	Original
Financial satisfaction	Irelan, Rabin, and Schwab (1987)	Original
Overall health	CSAHD (1978)	Original
Life satisfaction	CSAHD (1978)	Original
Mental health	CSAHD (1978)	Original
Sex role index	Bem (1974)	Modified
Attitudes on aging	Horowitz and Dobrof (1980)	Original
Familism index	Heller (1970)	Original
Familial attitudes	Horowitz and Dobrof (1980)	Original
Family relations	Horowitz and Dobrof (1980)	Original
Living arrangements	Horowitz and Dobrof (1980)	Original
Burden	Zarit, Reever, and Bach–Peterson (1980)	Modified
Dependence	Stryker (1955)	Modified
Relationship	Hudson (1982)	Modified
Relationship	Smilkstein (1978)	Modified

index mean and standard deviation were 1.93 and .63 respectively.

C. Task Competence Index. This index measures the degree to which caregivers feel competent in performing the range of tasks comprising the Task Frequency and Task Satisfaction Indices. This 22-item index is scored on a 4-point scale where 0 = not competent at all, 1 = not very competent, 2 = somewhat competent, and 3 = extremely competent. The reliability coefficient was .91. The index mean and standard deviation were 2.3 and .49 respectively.

Table A–2

Index Item Information and Reliability Analysis
(Standardized Item Alphas) for Composite Measures

Scale/Index Name	Number of Items	Reliability Coefficient
Task Frequency	22	.93 (MCG)
Task Satisfaction	22	.95 (MCG)
Task Competence	22	.91 (MCG)
Barriers to Caregiving	16	.86 (GLO)
		.86 (MCG)
Recipient Affection	5	.88 (MCG)
Provider Affection	5	.83 (MCG)
Family Function[a]	5	.85 (MCG)
Quality of Relationship[b]	5	.71 (MCG)
Service Receipt	12	.58 (MCG)
Service Need	12	.87 (MCG)
Illness[c]	21	.67 (MCG)
Activities of Daily Living[d]	15	.93 (MCG)
Behavioral Orientation	9	.79 (MCG)
Financial Health[f]	2	.76 (MCG)
Life Satisfaction[e]	4	.74 (MCG)
Sex Role[g]	10	.71 (MCG)
Familism[h]	8	.80 (MCG)
Burden[i]	10	.87 (MCG)

(MCG) = Male caregiver questionnaire
(GLO) = Group leader/organizer questionnaire

[a] = Smilkstein (1978)   [f] = Irelan, Rabin, and Schwab (1987)
[b] = Hudson (1982)   [g] = Bem (1974)
[c] = Shanas (1962)   [h] = Heller (1970)
[d] = Horowitz and Dobrof (1980)   [i] = Zarit, Reever, and Bach–Peterson (1980)
[e] = CSAHD (1978)

D. Barriers to Caregiving Index. This index gauges the extent to
which a range of potential factors serve to limit the amount of
care men provide to their relatives or friends. Both male caregiver respondents and group leader respondents were asked to
complete this index. Caregivers based their responses on their
personal experience of caregiving, and leaders based their responses on their group observations of the male caregiving experience. This 16-item index is scored on a 4-point scale where 0
= not at all, 1 = minimally, 2 = to some degree, and 3 = very
much so. The items included in the index are:

Table A–3

Summary Information on Factored Dimensions of Study Indices

Index Name	Factor/ Dimension	Number of Items	Reliability Coefficient
I. Task Frequency Index	1) Instrumental Daily Living Tasks (IDLT)	8	.91
	2) Functional Daily Living Tasks (FDLT)	6	.93
	3) Case Management Tasks (CMT)	5	.79
	4) Social Support Tasks (SST)	3	.75
II. Task Satisfaction Index	1) IDLT	8	.89
	2) FDLT	6	.91
	3) CMT	5	.86
	4) SST	3	.78
III. Task Competence Index	1) IDLT	8	.91
	2) FDLT	6	.92
	3) CMT	5	.85
	4) SST	3	.36
IV. Sex Role Index	1) Instrumental Orientation	4	.68
	2) Affective Orientation	4	.86
V. Barriers to Caregiving Index (GLO)	1) Physical/Emotional Health	6	.83
	2) Community/Family Support	6	.75
	3) Gender Related	4	.65
VI. Barriers to Caregiving Index (MCG)	1) Physical/Emotional Health	6	.77
	2) Community/Family Support	6	.61
	3) Gender Related	4	.75

(MCG) = Male caregiver questionnaire

(GLO) = Group leader/organizer questionnaire

1. The requirements of your job

2. Family obligations

3. The nature of your social life

4. Your opinion as to what appropriate behavior for men should be

5. The opinions of others as to what appropriate behavior for men should be

6. Quality of your past relations with your relative/friend

7. The general stress associated with caregiving

8. The distance you live from the relative/friend

9. The availability of other relatives and friends who can provide help

10. Your general health

11. The physical health of your relative/friend

12. The mental or emotional health of your relative/friend

13. The general personality of your relative/friend

14. The sex of your relative/friend

15. Your family's tradition of helping others

16. The availability of community services for your relative/friend

The reliability coefficient for male caregivers was .86. The reliability coefficient for group leaders was also .86. The index mean and standard deviation for male caregivers were .91 and .58, respectively, and 1.30 and .60 for leaders.

E. Recipient Affection Index. This index gauges the perceived level of affection expressed by elder recipients of care according to their male caregivers. This 5-item index is scored on a 5-point scale where 0 = rarely or never, 1 = seldom, 2 = sometimes, 3 = often, and 4 = almost always. The items included in the index are:

1. Listens to what is being said

2. Displays physical affection

3. Shows concern

4. Shows sympathy

5. Asks how the other is doing

The reliability coefficient was .88. The index mean and standard deviation were 1.86 and .99 respectively.

F. Provider Affection Index. This index is identical to the Recipient Affection Index except that the subject and object of affective expression have been reversed. This index gauges perceived levels of affection expressed by caregivers for care recipients. This index utilizes the same five items and 5-point scoring scale found in the Recipient Affection Index. The reliability coefficient was .83. The index mean and standard deviation were 3.10 and .67 respectively.

G. Family Function Index. This index, a modified version of the Family APGAR developed by Smilkstein (1978), gauges the male caregiver's level of satisfaction with the concern for him expressed by the elder care recipient. This 5-item index is scored on a 3-point scale where 1 = hardly ever, 2 = some of the time, and 3 = almost always. The items included in the index are:

1. I am satisfied with the help I receive from him/her when something is troubling me.

2. I am satisfied with the way the person I provide care for discusses items of common interest and shares problem solving with me.

3. I find the person I provide care for accepts my wishes for him/her to take on new activities and make changes in his/her life.

4. I am satisfied with the way he/she expresses affection and responds to my feelings such as anger, sorrow, and love.

5. I am satisfied with the way he/she and I share time together.

This index reflected a reliability coefficient of .85. The mean and standard deviation for this index were 1.79 and .60 respectively.

H. Quality of Relationship Index. This index, a shortened and modified version of the Index of Marital Satisfaction developed by Hudson (1982), gauges the degree of intimacy and affiliativeness between caregiver and care recipient. Utilizing a 4-point scale, this 5-item index is scored such that a 1 = rarely, or none of the time, 2 = a little of the time, 3 = a good part of the time, and 4 = most or all of the time (the points on the scale for items 1 and 2 (negative statements) were reversed prior to scoring). The five items comprising the index are:

1. I feel I cannot trust the person I provide care for.

2. I feel that our relationship is a poor one.

3. I feel that ours is a very close relationship.

4. I feel that we manage agreements and disagreements very well.

5. I feel that our relationship is very stable.

The reliability coefficient was .71. The mean score and standard deviation for this measure were 3.15 and .67 respectively.

I. Service Receipt Index. This index measures the extensiveness of the older person's community service support package. That is, it assesses the extent to which the care recipient benefits from formal organization services above and beyond those delivered by the male caregiver and other informal supports (i.e., relatives, friends, etc.). This 12-item index is scored on a 2-point scale such that a 0 = service not received and 1 = service received. The items in the index are:

1. Homemaker services

2. Home health aide services

3. Friendly visitor/telephone reassurance

4. Transportation/escort services

5. Home-delivered meals

6. Senior citizen center services

7. Adult day-care services

8. Counseling services

9. Physical therapy services

10. Visiting nurse services

11. Information and referral services

12. Hospital services

The reliability coefficient was .58. The mean and standard deviation were .12 and .14 respectively.

J. Service Need Index. The Service Need Index measures the extent to which caregivers perceived care recipients to be in need of a range of gerontological services. The same list of services included in the Service Receipt Index is represented in this index. This 12-item index is scored on a 2-point scale where 0 = service would not be used and 1 = service would be used. The reliability coefficient was .87. The mean and standard deviation were .18 and .25 respectively.

K. Illness Index. This index, developed by Shanas (1962), was slightly modified for this study. It gauges the range of health problems that care recipients suffered from according to their male caregivers. The Illness Index contains 21 items and is scored on a 2-point scale where 0 = the absence of the health problem and 1 = the presence of the health problem. The items in the Illness Index are:

1. Trouble hearing

2. Trouble seeing, even with glasses

3. A nagging cough

4. Diarrhea

5. Constipation

6. Feeling of dizziness

7. Headaches

8. Shortness of breath

9. Asthma

10. Losing weight for no reason

11. Arthritis or rheumatism

12. Diabetes

13. Stomach trouble

14. Gall bladder or liver trouble

15. Heart trouble

16. High blood pressure

17. Kidney trouble

18. Paralysis, any part of the body

19. Piles (hemorrhoids)

20. Sinus trouble

21. Varicose veins

The reliability coefficient was .67. The mean and standard deviation for this index were .14 and .12 respectively.

L. Activities of Daily Living Index. This index, developed by Horowitz and Dobrof (1982), is a modified version of a composite measure of instrumental and physical activities of daily living included in the OARS Multidimensional Functional Assessment Questionnaire (CSAHD, 1978). The Activities of Daily Living Index assesses the severity of impairment or restrictiveness in the care recipient's performance of daily activities. The index contains 15 items and is scored on a 3-point scale where 0 = no difficulty, 1 = some difficulty, and 2 = must have help. The items in the Activities of Daily Living Index are:

1. Use the telephone

2. Shop for groceries and other things

3. Get to places outside of walking distance

4. Prepare his/her own meals

5. Do light housework

6. Take his/her own medication

7. Handle his/her own money

8. Feed him/herself

9. Dress and undress him/herself

10. Care for his/her own appearance

11. Get about his/her house

12. Get up and down stairs

13. Bathe or shower him/herself

14. Get to the bathroom on time

15. Cut his/her toenails

The reliability coefficient was .93. The mean and standard deviation for this index were 1.53 and .47 respectively.

M. Behavioral Orientation Index. This index is based on a series of interviewer assessment questions included in the Older Americans Resources and Services (OARS) methodology (CSAHD, 1978). It assesses the caregiver's perception of the elder care recipient's degree of behavioral disturbance or mental impairment. This 9-item index is scored on a 3-point scale where 0 = rarely/never, 1 = occasionally, and 2 = often. The items in the Behavioral Orientation Index are:

1. Mentally confused and disoriented

2. Unpleasant and uncooperative

3. Depressed and/or tearful

4. Withdrawn or lethargic

5. Fearful, anxious, or extremely tense

6. Full of unrealistic physical complaints

7. Suspicious (more than reasonable)

8. Bizarre or inappropriate in thought or action

9. Excessively talkative or overly jovial or elated

The reliability coefficient was .79. The mean and standard deviation were .97 and .45 respectively.

N. Financial Health Index. This measure combines two questions from the Social Security Administration's Retirement History Survey (Irelan, Rabin, and Schwab 1987). This index gauges the caregivers' self-assessment of their state of financial satisfaction and security. The two questions comprising this measure are:

1. In your opinion, how well do you and other members of your household manage financially? Do you manage very well (1), fairly well (2), not very well (3), or poorly (4)?

2. Generally, how satisfied are you with the way you are living now—that is, as far as money and what you are able to have are concerned? Would you say the way you are living is: more than satisfactory (1), satisfactory (2), less than satisfactory (3), or very unsatisfactory (4)?

The reliability coefficient was .76. The mean and standard deviation were 1.88 and .57 respectively.

O. Life Satisfaction Index. This composite measure is comprised of four questions drawn from the OARS Methodology (CSAHD, 1978). The Life Satisfaction Index assesses the caregiver's perceived level of personal contentment in life. The four items in the index and their scoring values are:

1. How often do you feel lonely? Would you say very often (3), sometimes (2), rarely or never (1)?

2. How often would you say you worry about things—very often (3), fairly often (2), or hardly ever (1)?

3. In general, do you find life exciting (1), pretty routine (2), or dull (3)?

4. Taking everything into consideration, how would you describe your satisfaction with life in general at the present time—good (1), fair (2), or poor (3)?

The reliability coefficient was .74. The mean and standard deviation for the index were 2.08 and .27 respectively.

P. Sex Role Index. This index represents a modified and shortened version of Bem's (1974) sex-role inventory, which aims to measure psychological androgyny. The index gauges, as well, the extent to which individuals perceive themselves to exhibit traditional male (instrumental) as compared to female (affective) personality traits. The Sex Role Index is a 10-item composite measure scored on a 5-point scale where 1 = rarely or never, 2

= sometimes, 3 = often, 4 = usually, and 5 = almost always. The items in the index are:

1. Aggressive

2. Loving

3. Analytical

4. Compassionate

5. Forceful

6. Yielding

7. Competitive

8. Gentle

9. Self-sufficient

10. Warm

The reliability coefficient was .71. The mean and standard deviation for the index were 3.44 and .53 respectively.

Q. Familism Index. This index was previously developed by Heller (1970). It gauges the perceived strength of relationship and allegiance among members of the caregiver's family constellation. The eight statements in this index are scored on a 3-point scale where 1 = not at all, 2 = to some extent, and 3 = very much so. Items in the Familism Index are:

1. Members of my family are willing to share their homes with other family members.

2. Members of my family live close to each other so that mutual aid and cooperation might better be carried on.

3. Children in my family feel it is their responsibility to be with their parents in times of serious illness, even if they have moved some distance away.

4. Members of my family place family objectives above personal goals.

5. My family does not allow its common political and ethical views to be influenced by people outside the family.

6. As many activities as possible are shared by members of my family.

7. Whenever possible, members of my family talk over important life decisions (such as marriage, employment, residence) before taking action.

8. Members of my family feel morally obligated to pay medical bills which other members cannot pay.

The reliability coefficient was .80. The mean and standard deviation for the index were 1.94 and .45 respectively.

R. Burden Index. This composite measure of caregiver burden is a shortened version of Zarit, Reever, and Bach–Peterson's (1980) Burden Scale. The index aims to measure the extent to which male caregivers experience personal stress and strain during the course of caring for another person. The 10-item Burden Index is scored on a 5-point scale where 0 = never, 1 = rarely, 2 = sometimes, 3 = quite frequently, and 4 = nearly always. The statements comprising this measure are:

1. Do you feel that your relative/friend asks for more help than he/she needs?

2. Do you feel that because of the time you spend with your relative/friend that you don't have enough time for yourself?

3. Do you feel stressed between caring for your relative/friend and trying to meet other responsibilities for your family or work?

4. Do you feel that your relative currently affects your rela-

tionship with other family members or friends in a negative way?

5. Are you afraid what the future holds for your relative/friend?

6. Do you feel you don't have as much privacy as you would like because of your relative/friend?

7. Do you feel your health has suffered because of your involvement with your relative/friend?

8. Do you wish you could just leave the care of your relative/friend to someone else?

9. Do you feel uncertain about what to do about your relative/friend?

10. Overall, how often do you feel burdened in caring for your relative/friend?

The reliability coefficient was .87. The mean and standard deviation for this index were 1.71 and .77 respectively.

The Study Factors

A. Task Frequency Index Factors. Items in the Task Frequency Index underwent factor analysis, with four factors extracted and rotated with the varimax procedure. Summary information for these factors is presented in table A–3. Factor 1, labeled "Instrumental Daily Living Tasks" (IDLT), was defined by eight items—preparing meals, marketing or shopping, household cleaning, laundry, escort, help with medications, help with home repairs, and help with the telephone. Item loadings ranged from .49 to .87 on this factor. This dimension had an eigenvalue of 9.30 and accounted for 42.3 percent of the variance.

The second factor, labeled "Functional Daily Living Tasks" (FDLT), was defined by six items—help with dressing, help with shaving/brushing hair/applying ointments, help with eating meals, help with getting in and out of bed, help with going to the bathroom, and help with bathing. This factor had item loadings from .71 to .86. It had an eigenvalue of 2.21 and accounted for 10.1 percent of the variance.

Factor 3, labeled "Case Management Tasks" (CMT), was defined by five items—speaking at community agencies, arranging for outside services, supervising the help of relatives/friends, supervising the help of paid workers, and help with legal matters. Item loadings ranged from .68 to .77. This factor had an eigenvalue of 1.97 and accounted for 9.0 percent of the variance.

The fourth factor, labeled "Social Support Tasks" (SST), was defined by three items—providing companionship/emotional support, help with paying bills/writing checks, and help with writing letters/filling out forms. Items loaded from .56 to .86. This factor had an eigenvalue of 1.23 and explained 5.6% of the variance.

Cronbach alphas for the four factors were .91, .93, .79 and .75, respectively. Factor 1 had a mean score of 2.17 and a standard deviation of .91. Factor 2 had a mean score of 1.61 and a standard deviation of 1.12. Factor 3 had a mean and standard deviation of 1.67 and .87, respectively. Factor 4 emerged with a mean score of 2.66 and a standard deviation of .65.

B. Task Satisfaction Index Factors. As indicated earlier, the same four factors extracted from the Task Frequency Index were employed in the analysis of the Task Satisfaction Index. Cronbach's alphas for IDLT, FDLT, CMT, and SST were .89, .91, .86, and .78, respectively, reflecting moderate to high levels of reliability for the earlier derived factorial dimensions. Factor 1 reflected a mean of 2.00 and a standard deviation of .66. Factor 2 had a mean and standard deviation of 1.80 and .81 respectively. Factor 3 had a mean and standard deviation of 1.84 and .73, while Factor 4 had a mean of 2.13 and a standard deviation of .72.

C. Task Competence Index Factors. The four factors extracted from the Task Frequency Index were also employed in specialized analyses of the Task Competence Index. Cronbach alphas for IDLT, FDLT, CMT, and SST were .91, .92, .85, and .36, respectively, thus reflecting high levels of internal consistency for each of the earlier derived factors except Factor 4, Social Support Tasks. Continued application of the latter factorial dimension is deemed justified due to the limited number of items in this factor and the benefits of running comparative analyses on each factor across the three task performance indices. Factor 1 had a mean and standard deviation of 2.42 and .52 respectively. Factor 2 emerged with a composite mean and standard deviation of 1.94 and .87. Factor 3 had a mean of 2.31 and a standard deviation of .64, while Factor 4 reflected a mean of 2.62 and a standard deviation of .37.

D. Sex Role Index Factors. Items in the Sex Role Index also underwent factor analysis. In this case, two factorial dimensions containing two or more items were formulated. Table A–3 summarizes information about these factors. The first factor was characterized by traditional instrumental or male personality traits and is thus labeled "Instrumental Orientation." It contains four items—aggressive, analytical, forceful, and competitive. Item loadings for this factor ranged from .82 to .89. The eigenvalue for this factor was 3.16, with 31.6 percent of the variance explained. The reliability coefficient for this factor was .68. The mean and standard deviation were 3.99 and .75, respectively.

The second factor, labeled "Affective Orientation," contained four items indicative of traditional affective, female qualities— loving, compassionate, gentle, and warm. Item loadings ranged from .45 to .81. The reliability coefficient for this factorial dimension was .86. The mean and standard deviation were 2.87 and .82 respectively.

E. Barriers to Caregiving Index. This composite measure was administered to both male caregivers and caregiver support group leaders. Factor analysis was performed on the index completed by group leaders. Table A–3 summarizes the results. The first dimension, "Physical/Emotional Health," was defined by six items—the stress of caregiving, the availability of help from others, the caregiver's general health, the physical health of the care recipient, the mental health of the care recipient, and the personality of the care recipient. Items for this factor loaded from .61 to .77. This factor had an eigenvalue of 6.77 and explained 42.3 percent of the variance. The reliability coefficient for this factor was .83. The mean score and standard deviation were 1.73 and .71 respectively.

The second factor, labeled "Community/Family Support," was defined by six items—requirements of the job, family obligations, quality of past relations with the care recipient, distance lived from the care recipient, sex of the care recipient, and the availability of community services. Item loadings ranged from .45 to .84. This factor had an eigenvalue of 1.77 and explained 11.1 percent of the variance. This factor had a reliability coefficient of .75 and a mean and standard deviation of 1.22 and .74 respectively.

The third factor was labeled "Gender Related" and contained four items—the nature of the respondent's social life, his opinion of appropriate behavior for men, the opinion of others as to appropriate behavior of men, and his family's tradition of helping others. Items loaded from .46 to .88. This factor had an eigenvalue of 1.30 and explained 8.1 percent of the variance. Cronbach's alpha for this factor was .65. It had a mean and standard deviation of .75 and .61 respectively.

As was mentioned earlier, the three factors extracted from the Barriers to Caregiving Index administered to group leaders were utilized in analyzing male caregiver respondent data on a Barriers to Caregiving Index containing identical items. The reliability coefficients for the three factors in this case were .77, .61, and .75. The mean and standard deviation for the "Physical/Emotional Health" factor were 1.25 and .73 respectively. The mean and standard deviation for the "Community/Family Support" factor were .71 and .57 respectively. The mean and standard deviation on the "Gender-Related" factor were .74 and .75 respectively.

APPENDIX B
Practical Recommendations for Involving Men in Caregiver Support Groups*

How can we more successfully encourage caregiving males to reap the benefits of support group membership? The recommendations and ideas presented here represent a synthesis of findings drawn from the national study of the views and opinions of support group leaders and male group members engaged in elder caregiving. This material also incorporates the ideas of the study's expert panel. It is meant to serve as a practical guide for planning and operating caregiver support groups that are attuned to the special needs and concerns of men. It is intended to be used by support group leaders both to attract men to caregiver support groups and to address the concerns that they bring to these groups.

The Need for Help

Many men are reluctant to admit that they need outside assistance with caregiving tasks. Caregivers may trudge on under unbearable conditions rather than admit their perceived self-failure. What often happens in this situation is that the caregiver's own

*Geraldine McKenzie took responsibility for translating a series of technical study data into an earlier version of these practical program guidelines. Her assistance is gratefully acknowledged.

health suffers and he eventually needs care himself. In other cases, the caregiver doesn't realize that he is taking on too much until it is too late. The American Association of Retired Persons has identified the following danger signals to help caregivers recognize when they are approaching role overload and should seek outside help.

Danger Signals of Caregiver Overload

- Your relative's condition is worsening despite your best efforts.
- No matter what you do, it isn't enough.
- You feel you're the only person in the world enduring this.
- You no longer have any time or place to be alone for even a brief respite.
- Things you used to do occasionally to help out are now part of your daily routine.
- Family relationships are breaking down because of the caregiving pressures.
- Your caregiving duties are interfering with your work and social life to an unacceptable degree.
- You're going on in a no-win situation just to avoid admitting failure.
- You realize you're all alone—and doing it all—because you've shut out everyone who's offered help.
- You refuse to think of yourself because "that would be selfish" (even though you're unselfish 99 percent of the time).
- Your coping methods have become destructive: you're overeating or undereating, abusing drugs or alcohol, or taking it out on your relative.
- There are no more happy times: loving and caring have given way to exhaustion and resentment, and you no longer feel good about yourself or take pride in what you're doing.

The above list is reprinted with permission from *Modern Maturity*. Copyright 1988, American Association of Retired Persons.

In the past, men have participated in caregiver support groups in much lower numbers than women. In response to the question "In your opinion, what things most deter men from joining caregiver support groups?" our expert panel pointed to the following factors:

- Inability to leave care recipient.
- Lack of familiarity with support groups.
- Additional demands on already limited time.
- Fear of appearing or admitting they can't handle the situation.
- Reluctance to share personal feelings.
- Lack of other men in group.
- Inconvenient meeting time or location.
- Lack of identification with caregivers.
- Lack of clear cut benefits of groups.
- Pressures to be strong and independent.

These barriers to participation can be grouped into the three categories of structural barriers, socialization barriers, and marketing barriers. Ways to address these issues are discussed in the following sections.

Group Structure

Group organizers should give careful consideration to group structure before they begin to implement any plans. They should ask themselves what population am I trying to serve, and what characteristics will the group members have? The answers to these questions directly bear upon the group's structure, the frequency of meetings, the location of the meetings, and the type of group sponsorship.

Before choosing a group facilitator one must decide whether to use an individual or team approach. While most groups have one leader, there are several benefits of coleadership. With coleaders, one leader can focus on the presentation of information while the other concentrates on group dynamics. If a team is comprised of one male and one female leader, the likelihood increases that each group member will be able to relate to at least one of the leaders.

Personality and ability are also important in selecting group leaders. The leaders' style will bear directly on the functioning of the group members. The skills, qualities, and attributes that leaders should possess include:

- Emotional strength
- Nonthreatening manner
- Straightforward style
- Sense of humor
- Knowledge of concrete issues
- Empathy
- Previous experience as a caregiver
- Nonjudgmental attitude
- Knowledge of community resources
- Knowledge of cultural diversity and its implications for aging and caregiving
- Patience
- Understanding
- Organizational skills

Facilitators should be trained before they begin to lead a group. If they are not social workers or have no experience working with groups, they should be trained in group dynamics. They must know not only how to monitor and direct group process, but also be familiar with various types of personalities and how they influence groups.

One of the best ways to maintain a positive group process is to encourage group support. The facilitator should not try to take on too much of a leadership role. While group leaders should have a wealth of information and be sensitive to the concerns of group members, the caregivers themselves should interact and support each other as much as possible. It is best to avoid having one or two people monopolize the conversation. While some caregivers will speak more than others, the facilitators should intercede when someone dominates the group.

The group process should be a positive one; the meetings should not slip too far into negativism. While caregiving can be depressing or demoralizing, meetings that do not focus the group members' energies on positive ends will quickly lose the caregivers' interest.

Group leaders should also be trained in the differences between counseling men and women, male development and socialization, the aging process, entitlements and benefits, and community resources. They should also be sensitized to the customs and traditions of racial and ethnic groups residing within the community.

Group Membership

Most caregiver support groups are open to any caregiver who wants to participate. In the past few years, however, there has been movement toward the creation of groups that restrict their membership to persons who meet certain criteria. Part of the impetus behind this movement is the belief that group members are able to relate better to similar people. For example, male caregivers may relate better to male caregivers, and employed caregivers may relate better to employed caregivers.

The results of the present study indicate, however, that homogeneity among group members is not very important. Group members often benefit from hearing about the experiences of other kinds of people. They learn new coping strategies and are exposed to people who have different skills and are familiar with different resources. For group members who are caring for persons with senile dementia, it is beneficial for them to share with caregivers who are dealing with different stages of the disease. They learn not only what to expect in the future, but are able to assist those whose impaired elders are just beginning to display symptoms.

Regarding gender, homogeneity also seems to be relatively unimportant. Group leaders report that group functioning is not affected by gender. Neither sex dominates the group or expresses greater satisfaction or dissatisfaction with group activities. Men report that they feel comfortable sharing their thoughts and feelings with the group. They do not participate any more or less than the women in the group do.

Sponsorship

The auspices under which the support group operates will effect both the number and type of caregivers who come to the meetings. Group organizers should determine whom they hope to serve, and then select the type of sponsorship that will be most attractive to that particular group. The most common types of sponsorship are corporate, community agency, church or synagogue, social or fraternal organization, and organizational co-sponsorship (corporation and community agency, for example). It is critical for group organizers to evaluate whether sponsorship will positively or negatively bear on the male caregiver's decision to attend the support group. The following questions should be used to evaluate the impact of the potential sponsors:

- Is the organization highly regarded within the community?
- Will caregivers feel comfortable associating with the organization?
- Is it a neutral body?

Every effort should be made to ensure that male caregivers are not deterred from the group because of its affiliation with a particular sponsor.

Group Size

The optimal size of the group depends upon the group's purpose. Most traditional support groups have a membership of eight to twenty people. This is small enough to encourage people to open up, yet large enough for people to share the responsibility of maintaining discussion.

Groups whose primary purpose is to provide general, concrete information can maintain a much larger membership.

Lecture-style meetings will meet the needs of many caregivers. They will not, however, meet the needs of those caregivers who are looking for emotional support or individualized attention.

Meeting Time

Selection of the meeting time and session length of the support group is significant. Most support group meetings range from one to two-and-a-half hours in length. Included in this time is pre- or postmeeting socialization, a time for attendees to mingle with other caregivers.

The time of the meetings must be carefully selected to appeal to the type of caregiver targeted for participation. Older caregivers often prefer daytime meetings, because they are more comfortable driving or walking during the day, and because formal respite services are more accessible during daytime hours. Evening meetings are most appropriate for men who work and for those caregivers who depend on working families' members for transportation and/or respite.

The frequency with which the group meets is also dependent upon the group's composition and functioning. Most support groups have monthly meetings. Lecture-style groups often meet bimonthly. Time-limited (six sessions, for example) informational series often meet weekly. Weekly meetings are appropriate for caregivers who are not burdened with the responsibility of obtaining respite care. Meetings can quickly become a chore for people who have difficulty leaving their dependent elder.

Location of Meeting

Group meetings should be held at a central site that is easily accessible by both public and private transportation. The meeting room should be wheelchair accessible, well lit, and large enough to comfortably accommodate the group. The most frequently used facilities for caregiver support group meetings are public buildings (such as libraries and municipal buildings), facilities for the aged, churches or synagogues, community service buildings, and group members' homes.

Format

The format of most support group meetings consists of several different activities, including:

- Information sharing
- Personal sharing
- Mutual support time
- Problem solving
- Guest speakers
- Socializing

Generally, male caregivers are satisfied with meetings that include these components. A frequent request is for the provision of practical information to be a primary part of the meetings.

Marketing the Group

It is important to remember that marketing includes outreach. Generally, men are less likely to attend groups of this nature than are women. Many male caregivers, particularly those over the age of fifty, were socialized to believe that they must be strong, proud, and independent. Throughout their lives they have striven for self-sufficiency and have avoided asking for or accepting help from outsiders. Different strategies may be employed by support group leaders to combat the feeling of failure that some men associate with the need for a support group. The group should be marketed in a professional manner, with stress on expert advice and the provision of concrete information in the marketing campaign. Language that is acceptable to men should be used to describe the group's process. Benefits should be emphasized such as community resources, legal and financial information, information dissemination, and expert speakers. The following techniques are suggested for increasing the group's appeal to men:

- Including men in the outreach.
  Many men believe that support groups are for women.

They also fear that they will be the only male in the group if they do attend. Including men in newspaper articles, public service announcements, and television ads will tell men directly and indirectly that support groups are for them.

- Utilizing a credible male spokesperson.
  Men have been socialized to "bear up" and "be tough." They are reluctant to admit that they can't handle a situation. A respected male figure will add credibility to the support group. He will give men someone strong to identify with.

- Focus on the provision of concrete information.
  Men will frequently be more responsive to a program that offers practical information than to one which focuses on emotional support. Informational seminars should be used to bring men to the support group. They will likely be more accepting of other aspects of the caregiver support group after they are exposed to its structure and membership.

- Having male group members contact other male caregivers.
  Again, many men are reluctant to attend a meeting that they think will be dominated by women. Male recruiters can reduce prospective apprehensions and help them to adjust to the group.

Other marketing strategies that can be used to attract both men and women to the support group include:

- Notices on community bulletin boards
- Newspaper articles
- Notices on community calendars
- Public service announcements—radio and television
- Brochure distribution
- Announcements in church or synagogue bulletins
- Presentations to social, fraternal, and civic organizations
- Personal contact with referral sources

- Listings in community resource directories
- Booths at community fairs
- Posters
- Targeted mailings
- Lunchtime seminars and corporate breakfasts
- Union and industry newsletters

Various combinations of these techniques should be used to publicize the group. Leaders should not depend on a single method of outreach.

The benefits of a support group may not be evident to those who are unfamiliar with such programs. The two hours that are spent at the group may appear to be a burden or a waste of time to many busy caregivers. To combat these negative impressions, educational information should be stressed in press releases. A newsletter can be sent to a targeted group of likely male caregivers. Along with an advertisement of the group's meetings, the tangible benefits of the group should be listed. The meeting as a place to gain as well as to give should be advertised. A male member should contact potential new members and stress the positive benefits of the group. Through discussion of the many tasks that fall within the realm of caregiving, the general public will become educated about the aging process and the demands of caregiving.

Group Meeting Content

Caregivers seek a wide variety of information from support groups. The following list outlines the topics that are most commonly covered in support group meetings.

- Practical Information
    Legal issues
    Accessing community resources
    Combining formal and informal services
    Stages of Alzheimer's disease
    Normal and abnormal aging
    Respite care

      Entitlements
      Relinquishing home care for institutional care
      Housing options
      Home safety

- Skill Development
      Household tasks
      Balancing responsibilities
      Provision of personal care
      How to ask for and accept help
      Techniques for handling problematic situations
      Time management
      Long-distance caregiving
      Decision making
      Case management
      Administration of medications and health care

- Emotional and Social Issues
      Coping with death and dying
      Preparing for widowhood
      Dealing with personality conflicts
      Family relations
      Taking care of one's self
      Leisure time
      Dealing with social or sexual deprivation
      Understanding and accepting role reversal
      Maintaining self-esteem
      Appropriate expressions of anger

Many older adults and their families have a difficult time choosing the amount and type of health insurance that is appropriate for their needs. Both over- and underinsured elders need assistance in evaluating their coverage. Older persons and their caregivers should be encouraged to examine their insurance policies to ensure that they have sufficient coverage without unnecessary duplication.

Unless a group leader or a member of the group has extensive knowledge of the subject, an expert should be invited to a meeting to discuss health insurance. Medicare handbooks, which can be obtained from local Social Security offices, should also be distributed to caregivers. Other key issues currently facing care-givers include long-term care, Medicaid eligibility and rules, home health care, and supplemental health and insurance poli-cies.

It is important to make caregivers aware of the various serv-ices and programs that are available to assist them. The fol-lowing services are likely to be available in the community and should be reviewed periodically:

- home health care services
- congregate meals programs or home delivered meals
- friendly visitor programs
- adult day care
- hospice services
- telephone reassurance
- homemaker or chore services
- respite care
- transportation programs
- senior centers
- counseling/family service programs
- escort and shopping assistance services

Resources: Publications and Guidebooks

Alzheimer's Family Support Groups: A Manual for Group Facilitators
Suncoast Gerontology Center
University of South Florida Medical Center
12901 N. 30th Street
Box 50
Tampa, FL 33612

Caregiving Tips: Taking Care of Yourself, How to Find and Use Community Services, Living Arrangements, Options for the Frail Elderly

Family Caregivers Program
National Council on the Aging, Inc.
600 Maryland Avenue S.W.
West Wing 100
Washington, DC 20024

Caring: A Family Guide to Managing Alzheimer's Patients at Home
Fund for Aging Services—Alzheimer's Disease
New York City Alzheimer's Disease Resource Center
280 Broadway
New York, NY 10007

Development, Implementation, and Operation of Family Support Groups
Christopher L. Hayes, Ph.D.
Center for the Study of Pre-Retirement and Aging
The Catholic University of America
Washington, DC 20064

Families of the Aged
CD Publications
100 Summit Building
8555 16th Street
Silver Springs, MD 20910-2889

Family Seminars for Caregiving: A Facilitator's Guidebook
University Press
University of Washington
JA-20
Seattle, WA 98195

Hand in Hand: Learning from and Caring for Older Parents
AARP Books
Scott Foreman and Company
Dept. HHB
400 S. Edward Street
Mt. Prospect, IL 60056

Idea Book on Caregiver Support Groups
National Council on the Aging, Inc.
600 Maryland Avenue S.W.
West Wing 100
Washington, DC 20024

*Information for Caregivers of the Elderly: Resource Manual
    and Instructor's Manual*
S. Bane and B. Halpert
Center on Aging Studies
University of Missouri
Kansas City, MO 64110

In Support of Caregivers
The Vocational Studies Center
University of Wisconsin–Madison
964 Educational Sciences Building
1025 W. Johnson Street
Madison, WI 53706

Starting a Self-Help Group for Caregivers of the Elderly
Children of Aging Parents
2761 Trenton Road
Levittown, PA 19056

*Support Groups for Caregivers of the Aged: A Training
    Manual for Facilitators*
H. Rzeteleny and J. Mellor
Brookdale Center on Aging
Hunter College
New York, NY 10022

The Aging Parent
The American Jewish Committee
Institute of Human Relations
165 E. 56th Street
New York, NY 10022

Wellsprings: A Training Program for Family Caregivers
Graduate School of Social Work
University of Utah
Salt Lake City, UT 84112

Resources: Organizations

Alzheimer's Disease and Related Disorders Association, Inc.
70 East Lake Street
Chicago, IL 60601

American Association of Homes for the Aging
1129 20th Street N.W.
Suite 400
Washington, DC 20036

American Association of Retired Persons
1909 K Street N.W.
Washington, DC 20049

Children of Aging Parents
2761 Trenton Road
Levittown, PA 19056

National Association of Area Agencies on Aging
600 Maryland Avenue S.W.
Suite 208
Washington, DC 20024

National Association for Home Care
519 C Street N.E.
Stanton Park
Washington, DC 20002

The Eldercare Connection
The Partnership Group, Inc.
840 West Main Street
Lansdale, PA 19446

APPENDIX C
Glossary of Statistical Terms Used in This Book

We have made a concerted effort in this book to minimize reference to statistical terminology in the hopes of maximizing the readability and immediate application of this work for professionals at all levels of the gerontological services network. Even so, any book which reports on the conduct of research cannot avoid including reference to certain methodological and statistical procedures which were employed during the course of activities. This "nontechnical" glossary of terms is being offered for the purpose of clarifying the meaning of certain statistical procedures referred to in the text. Every effort has been made to keep the explanations simple and brief—therefore these are not to be considered complete definitions. Statistical formulas have not been included. We hope those readers who do not generally engage in research initiatives find this glossary helpful.

ANOVA (Analysis of variance) (F): A statistical procedure in which differences in scores on a dependent variable are assessed for different categories or subgroups (3 or more usually) of an independent variable. The statistic produced is the F ratio. The higher the F score the greater the difference or variance in scores across the subgroups.

Beta coefficient: The beta coefficient is used in regression analysis to assess which independent variables are most useful in explaining changes in the dependent variable. The higher the beta, the stronger the relationship between the independent and dependent variables.

Chronbach's alpha: See coefficient alpha.

Coefficient alpha (α): A statistic measuring the internal consistency of the items comprising an index or scale. The higher the α the greater the consistency of the items.

Correlation coefficient (r): A statistic which reflects the strength of the association or relationship between two variables. The higher the r the stronger the relationship.

Descriptive statistics: Statistics which describe the basic characteristics of a sample (e.g., frequencies and percentages).

Eigenvalue: In factor analysis, a measure of the variance of each factor. Higher eigenvalues reflect more variance explained by a particular subgrouping of variables or items in an index.

Factor analysis: A statistical method for arriving at the dominant characteristics and their associated variables underlying multiple item indices. A factor analysis produces subgroupings of variables or items in an index reflecting a common characteristic or dimension.

Mean: The average score.

N: Sample size.

Pearson's (product-moment) correlation: See correlation coefficient.

Probability (p): A statistical procedure which determines the frequency with which a particular value of a variable is likely to occur. The lower the p the lesser the likelihood that a particular value occurred by chance.

R²: A measure of strength of association between a dependent and independent variables in regression analysis. A higher R^2 denotes a stronger association between variables.

Reliability coefficient: See coefficient alpha.

SPSS-X: A statistical computer sofware package available for mainframes, microcomputers, and personal computers.

Standard deviation (S.D.): The extent to which individual observations vary from the average observation on a particular variable. The higher the S.D. the more heterogeneity there is in the population.

Stepwise Multiple Regression Analysis: A statistical procedure for analyzing the relationships among several variables simultaneously. A series of independent variables believed to effect the dependent variable are considered in different combinations in this procedure. Statistics which are produced in this analysis include the beta and the R^2. Each represents a measure of the extent to which one or more independent variables effect the dependent variable.

t test (t): A statistical procedure in which differences in scores on a dependent variable are assessed for the subgroups of a dichotomous (two value) independent variable. The higher the t the greater the likelihood that the difference between subgroups did not occur by chance.

REFERENCES

Applegate, J.S. (1987). Beyond the dyad: Including the father in separation–individuation. *Child and Adolescent Social Work Journal* 4:92–105.

Bakan, D. (1966). *The duality of human existence.* Chicago: Rand McNally.

Barnett, R.C., and Baruch, G.K. (1987). Social roles, gender, and psychological distress. In R.C. Barnett, L. Biener, and G.K. Baruch (Eds.), *Gender and stress* (pp. 122–143). New York: The Free Press.

Barrow, G.M. (1986). *Aging, the individual and society* (3rd ed.). St. Paul: West Publishing Co.

Barry, H., Bacon, M.K., and Child, I.L. (1957). A cross-cultural survey of some sex differences in socialization. *Journal of Abnormal and Social Psychology* 55:327–332.

Barusch, A.S., and Spaid, W.M. (1989). Gender differences in caregiving: Why do wives report greater burden? *The Gerontologist* 29:667–676.

Beck, M. (1989, October). The geezer boom. *Newsweek Special Issue: The 21st Century Family.* pp. 62–68.

Belenky, M.F., Clinchy, B.M., Goldberger, N.R., and Tarule, J.M. (1986). *Women's ways of knowing.* New York: Basic Books.

Bem, S.L. (1974). The measurement of psychological androgyny. *Journal of Consulting and Clinical Psychology* 42:155–162.

Block, J. (1984). *Sex role identity and ego development.* San Francisco: Jossey Bass.

Boles, J., and Tatro, C. (1982). Androgyny. In K. Solomon and N.B. Levy (Eds.), *Men in transition: Theory and therapy* (pp. 99–129). New York: Plenum Press.

Bowers, B.J. (1987). Intergenerational caregiving: Adult caregivers and their aging parents. *Advanced Nursing Science* 9:20–31.

Brody, E.M. (1981). Women in the middle and family help to older people. *The Gerontologist* 21:471–480.

Brody, E.M. (1985). Parent care as a normative family stress. *The Gerontologist* 25:19–29.

Brody, E.M. (1986). Filial care of the elderly and changing roles of women (and men). *Journal of Geriatric Psychiatry* 19:175–201.

Cantor, M.H. (1983). Strain among caregivers: A study of experience in the United States. *The Gerontologist* 23:597–604.

Caregiving's toll: Employees run late. (1989, October). *AARP Bulletin* 30:13.

Cath, S.H. (1983). [Review of sex differences in coping and perceptions of life events]. *Journal of Geriatric Psychiatry* 16:211–222.

Cath, S.H., Gurwitt, A.R., and Ross, J.M. (Eds.) (1982). *Father and child: Developmental and clinical perspectives.* Boston: Little, Brown.

Center for the Study of Aging and Human Development [CSAHD]. (1978). *The OARS Methodology* (2nd ed.). Durham, N.C.: Author.

Chodorow, N. (1978). *The reproduction of mothering: Psychoanalysis and the sociology of gender.* Berkeley, Calif.: University of California Press.

Davies, H., Priddy, J.M., and Tinklenberg, J.R. (1986). Support groups for male caregivers of Alzheimer's patients. *Clinical Gerontologist* 5:385–395.

Fischer, L.R., and Eustis, N.N. (1988). DRGs and family care for the elderly. *The Gerontologist* 28:383–389.

Fitting, M., and Rabins, P. (1985). Men and women: Do they give care differently? *Generations* 10:23–26.

Fitting, M., Rabins, P., Lucas, M.J., and Eastham, J. (1986). Caregivers for dementia patients: A comparison of husbands and wives. *The Gerontologist* 26:248–252.

George, L.K. (1984). The burden of caregiving: How much? What kinds? For whom? *Center Reports on Advances in Caregiving* 8:1–8.

George, L.K. and Gwyther, L.P. (1986). Caregiver well-being: A multi-dimensional examination of family caregivers of demented adults. *The Gerontologist* 26:253–259.

Gilhooly, M.L.M. (1984). The impact of care-giving on care-givers: Factors associated with the psychological well-being of people supporting a demented relative in the community. *British Journal of Medical Psychology* 57:35–44.

Gilligan, C. (1982). *In a different voice.* Cambridge, Mass.: Harvard University Press.

Gutmann, D. (1987). *Reclaimed powers: Toward a new psychology of men and women in later life.* New York: Basic Books.

Graham, H. (1983). Caring: A labour of love. In J. Finch and D. Groves (Eds.), *A labour of love: Women, work and caring.* London: Routledge and Kegan Paul.

Gwyther, L.P., and George, L.K. (1986). Introduction to symposium: Caregivers for dementia patients: Complex determinants of well-being and burden. *The Gerontologist* 26:245–247.

Hartman, A. (1981). The family: A central focus for practice. *Social Work* 26:7–13.

Heller, P.L. (1970). Familism Scale: A measure of family solidarity. *Journal of Marriage and the Family* 32:73–80.

Hlavaty, J.P. (1986, April). *Alzheimer's disease and the male spouse caregiver.* Paper presented at the 10th Annual Professional and Scientific Ohio Conference on Aging, Columbus, Ohio.

Hooyman, N.R., and Lustbader, W. (1986). *Taking care: Supporting older people and their families.* New York: The Free Press.

Horowitz, A. (1985a). Family caregiving to the frail elderly. In M.P. Lawton and G. Maddox (Eds.), *The Annual Review of Gerontology and Geriatrics 5* (pp. 194–246). New York: Springer.

Horowitz, A. (1985b). Sons and daughters as caregivers to older parents: Differences in role performance and consequences. *The Gerontologist* 25:612–617.

Horowitz, A., and Dobrof, R. (1980, November). *The impact of caring for an elderly relative.* Paper presented at the 33rd Annual Scientific Meeting of the Gerontological Society of America, San Diego, Calif.

Horowitz, A., and Shindelman, L.W. (1983). Reciprocity and affection: Past influences on current caregiving. *Journal of Gerontological Social Work* 5:5–20.

Hudson, W.W. (1982). *The clinical measurement package: A field manual.* Chicago: Dorsey Press.

Irelan, L.M., Rabin, W., and Schwab, K. (1987). *Social Security Administration's Retirement History Study: Technical Description.* Washington, D.C.: U.S. Government Printing Office.

Jackson, J.S. (1989). Race, ethnicity, and psychological theory and research. *Journal of Gerontology: Psychological Sciences* 44:1–2.

Johnson, C. (1983). Dyadic family relations and social support. *The Gerontologist* 23:377–383.

Johnson, C. (1985). The impact of illness on late-life marriages. *Journal of Marriage and the Family* 47:156–217.

Johnson, C., & Catalano, D. (1983). A longitudinal study of family supports to impaired elderly. *The Gerontologist* 23:612–618.

Kane, R.A. (1985). A family caregiving policy: Should we have one? *Generations* 10:33–36.

Kaye, L.W. (1988). Generational equity: Pitting young against old. *New England Journal of Human Services* 8:8–11.

Kaye, L.W., and Applegate, J.S. (1990). Men as elder caregivers: A response to changing families. *American Journal of Orthopsychiatry* 60:86–95.

Kaye, L.W., and Applegate, J.S. (in press). Men as elder caregivers: Building a research agenda for the 1990s. *Journal of Aging Studies*.

Levinson, D.J., Darrow, C.N., Klein, E.B., Levinson, M.H., and McKee, B. (1978). *The seasons of a man's life.* New York: Ballantine Books.

Lewis, R.A., and Roberts, C.L. (1982). Postparental fathers in distress. In K. Solomon and N.B. Levy (Eds.), *Men in transition: Theory and therapy* (pp. 199–204). New York: Plenum Press.

Linsk, N.L., Keigher, S.M. and Osterbusch, S.E. (1988). States' policies regarding paid family caregiving. *The Gerontologist* 28:204–212.

Liptzin, B. (1984). [Discussion of elderly men as caregivers of wives]. *Journal of Geriatric Psychiatry* 17:61–68.

Livson, F.B. (1983). Gender identity: A life-span view of sex-role development. In R.B. Weg (Ed.), *Sexuality in the later years: Roles and behavior* (pp. 105–127). New York: Academic Press.

Longino, C.F. (1988). Who are the oldest Americans? *The Gerontologist* 28:515–523.

Lowenthal, M.F., Thurnher, M., and Chiriboga, D. (1975). *Four stages of life: A comparative study of women and men facing transitions.* San Francisco: Jossey–Bass.

Lowy, L. (1986). The implications of demographic trends as they affect the elderly. *Journal of Geriatric Psychiatry* 19:149–174.

McAuley, W.J., and Arling, B. (1984). Use of in-home care by very old people. *Journal of Health and Social Behavior* 25:54–64.

Miller, B. (1987). Gender and control among spouses of the cognitively impaired: A research note. *The Gerontologist* 27:447–453.

Montgomery, R.J.V., and Kamo, Y. (1987, November). *Differences between sons and daughters in parental caregiving.* Paper presented at the 40th Annual Scientific Meeting of the Gerontological Society of America, Washington, D.C.

Moore, D. (1983, January 30). America's neglected elderly. *The New York Times Magazine*, pp. 30–35.

Moritz, D.J., Kasl, S.V., and Berkman, L.F. (1989). The health impact of living with a cognitively impaired spouse: Depressive symptoms and social functioning. *Journal of Gerontology: Social Sciences* 44:S17–27.

Morycz, R.K. (1985). Caregiving strain and the desire to institutionalize family members with Alzheimer's disease: Possible predictors and model development. *Research on Aging* 7:329–361.

Motenko, A.K. (1988). Respite care and pride in caregiving: The experience of six older men caring for their disabled wives. In S. Reinharz and G.D. Rowles (Eds.), *Qualitative Gerontology* (pp. 104–127). New York: Springer.

Motenko, A.K. (1989). The frustrations, gratifications, and well-being of dementia caregivers. *The Gerontologist* 29:166–172.

Mothers bearing a second burden. (1989, May 14). *The New York Times*, p. 14.

National Council on Aging [NCOA]. (1985). *State support for respite care: Report of an exploratory survey.* Washington, D.C.: Author.

Neugarten, B.L. (Ed.). (1968). *Middle age and aging.* Chicago: Chicago University Press.

Noelker, L.S., and Bass, D.M. (1989). Home care for elderly persons: Linkages between formal and informal caregivers. *Journal of Gerontology: Social Sciences* 44:S63–70.

Older Women's League [OWL]. (1987). *Till death do us part: Caregiving wives of severly disabled husbands.* Washington, D.C.: Author. (Original version published 1982).

O'Neil, J.M. (1982). Gender-role conflict and strain in men's lives. In K. Solomon and N.B. Levy (Eds.), *Men in transition: Theory and therapy* (pp. 5–44). New York: Plenum Press.

Opinion Research Corporation. (1989). *A National Survey of Caregivers: Working Caregivers Report.* Washington, D.C.: American Association of Retired Persons.

Palliat, P. (1976). Bureaucratization of old age: Determinants of the process, possible safeguards, and reorientation. In E. Shanas and M.B. Sussman (Eds.), *Family, bureaucracy, and the elderly* (pp. 60–74). Durham, N.C.: Duke University Press.

Parsons, J., and Bales, R.F. (1955). *Family socialization and interaction process.* New York: Free Press of Glencoe.

Pedersen, F.A. (Ed.). (1980). *The father–infant relationship: Observational studies in the family setting.* New York: Praeger.

Pratt, C., Schmall, V., and Wright, S. (1987). Ethical concerns of family caregivers to dementia patients. *The Geronlologist* 27:632–638.

Pratt, C., Wright, S., and Schmall, V. (1987). Burden, coping and health status: A comparison of family caregivers to community dwelling and institutionalized Alzheimer's patients. *Journal of Gerontological Social Work* 10:99–112.

Pruchno, R.A., and Resch, N.L. (1989). Husbands and wives as caregivers: Antecedents of depression and burden. *The Gerontologist* 29:159–165.

Pruett, K.D. (1987). *The nurturing father.* New York: Warner Books.

Purvis, A. (1989, November 20). Alzheimer's rise. *Time.* 118.

Quayhagen, M.P., and Quayhagen, M. (1988). Alzheimer's stress: Coping with the caregiving role. *The Gerontologist* 28:391–396.

Rathbone–McCuan, E., and Coward, R.T. (1985, November). *Male helpers: Unrecognized informal supports.* Paper presented at the 38th Annual Scientific Meeting of the Gerontological Society of America, New Orleans, La.

Rowles, G.D., and Reinharz, S. (1988). Qualitative gerontology: Themes and challenges. In S. Reinharz and G.D. Rowles (Eds.), *Qualitative Gerontology* (pp. 3–33). New York: Springer.

Scharlach, A.E., and Boyd, S.L. (1989). Caregiving and employment: Results of an employee survey. *The Gerontologist* 29:382–387.

Schick, F.L. (1986). *Statistical handbook on aging Americans.* Phoenix: Onyx Press.

Seltzer, M.M., Ivry, J., and Litchfield, L.C. (1987). Family members as case managers: Partnership between the formal and informal support networks. *The Gerontologist* 27:722–728.

Shanas, E. (1979). The family as a social support system in old age. *The Gerontologist* 19:169–174.

Shanas, E. (1962). *The health of older people: A social survey.* Cambridge, Mass.: Harvard University Press.

Shanas, E. (1984). Old parents and middle-aged children: The four- and five-generation family. *Journal of Geriatric Psychiatry* 17:7–19.

Shanas, E., Townsend, P., Wedderburn, D., Fritis, H., Milhoj, P., and Strehouwer, J. (1968). *Old people in three industrial societies.* New York: Atherton Press.

Sheehan, N.W., and Nuttall, P. (1988). Conflict, emotion, and personal strain among family caregivers. *Family Relations* 37:92–98.

Sherman, S.R., Ward, R.A., and LaGory, M. (1988). Women as caregivers of elderly: Instrumental and expressive support. *Social Work* 33:164–167.

Sinnott, J.D. (1984). Older men, older women: Are their perceived sex roles similar? *Sex Roles* 10:847–857.

Smilkstein, G. (1978). The family APGAR: A proposal for a family function test and its use by physicians. *Journal of Family Practice* 6:1231–1239.

Snyder, B., and Keefe, K. (1985). The unmet needs of family caregivers for frail and disabled adults. *Social Work in Health Care* 10:1–14.

Solomon, K. (1982). The older man. In K. Solomon and N.B. Levy (Eds.), *Men in transition: Theory and therapy* (pp. 205–240). New York: Plenum.

Sommers, T. (1985). Caregiving: A women's issue. *Generations* 10:9–13.

Stoller, E.P. (1983). Parent caregiving by adult children: *Journal of Marriage and the Family* 45:851–858.

Stoller, E.P. (1985). Elder-caregiver relationship in shared households. *Research on Aging* 7:175–193.

Stoller, E.P., and Earl, L.L. (1983). Help with activities of everyday life: Sources of support for the noninstitutionalized elderly. *The Gerontologist* 23:64–70.

Stoller, E.P. and Pugliesi, K.L. (1989). The transition to the caregiving role: A panel study of helpers of elderly people. *Research on Aging* 11:312–330.

Stone, R., Cafferata, G.L., and Sangl, J. (1987). Caregivers of the frail elderly: A national profile. *The Gerontologist* 27:616–626.

Stryker, S. (1955). Attitude ascription in adult married offspring-parent relationships: A study of implications of the social psychological theory of G.H. Mead. Ph.D. dissertation. University of Minnesota.

Stueve, A., and O'Donnell, L. (1989). Interactions between women and their elderly parents: Constraints of daughters' employment. *Research on Aging* 11:331–353.

Sussman, M.B. (1985). The family life of old people. In R.H. Binstock and E. Shanas (Eds.), *Handbook of aging and the social sciences* (2nd. Ed.), (pp. 415–449). New York: Van Nostrand Reinhold.

Sussman, M.B., and Cogswell, B.E. (1972). The meaning of variant and experimental marriage styles and family forms in the 1970s. *Family Coordinator* 21:375–381.

Tennstedt, S.L., McKinlay, J.B., and Sullivan, L.M. (1989). Informal care for frail elders: The role of secondary caregivers. *The Gerontologist* 29:677–683.

Troll, L.E., Miller, S.J., and Atchley, R.C. (1979). *Families in later life*. Belmont, Calif.: Wadsworth.

U.S. Bureau of the Census. (1989). Projections of the population of the United States, by age, sex, and race: 1988 to 2080. *Current Popu-*

lation Reports, Series P–25, No. 1018. Washington, D.C.: U.S. Government Printing Office.

Vinick, B.H. (1984). Elderly men as caregivers of wives. *Journal of Geriatric Psychiatry* 17:61–68.

Weinstein, G.W. (1989, October). Help wanted—The crisis of elder care. *Ms.* pp. 73–79.

Winogrand, I.R., Fisk, A.A., Kirsling, R.A., and Keyes, B. (1987). The relationship of caregiver burden and morale to Alzheimer's disease patient function in a therapeutic setting. *The Gerontologist* 27:336–339.

Wood, J. (1987). Labors of love. *Modern Maturity* 30:28–34.

Young, R.F., and Kahana, E. (1989). Specifying caregiver outcomes: Gender and relationship aspects of caregiving strain. *The Gerontologist* 29:660–666.

Zarit, J.M. (1982). *Predictors of burden and distress for caregivers of senile dementia patients*. Unpublished doctoral dissertation, University of Southern California, Los Angeles, Calif.

Zarit, S., Reever, K., and Bach–Peterson, J. (1980). Relatives of the impaired elderly: Correlates of feelings of burden. *The Gerontologist* 20:649–655.

Zarit, S., Todd., P.A., and Zarit, J.M. (1986). Subjective burden of husbands and wives as caregivers: A longitudinal study. *The Gerontologist* 26:260–266.

Index

About the Authors

Lenard W. Kaye, associate professor at the Bryn Mawr College Graduate School of Social Work and Social Research, received his M.S.W. at New York University School of Social Work and his doctorate at the Columbia University School of Social Work. The former associate director of the Brookdale Institute on Aging and Adult Human Development and faculty member at Columbia University School of Social Work, he is co-author of *Resolving Grievances in the Nursing Home.* Dr. Kaye is also co-author of the forthcoming book *Geriatric Case Practice in Home Health Care* and is currently co-editing *Congregate Housing for the Elderly.* He has published widely on issues in nursing home advocacy, home health care, retirement lifestyles, and long-term care. Dr. Kaye sits on the editorial boards of the *Journal of Gerontological Social Work* and *Research on Social Work Practice* and is a fellow of the Gerontological Society of America.

A native midwesterner, **Jeffrey S. Applegate** received his bachelor's and master's degrees in social work from Indiana University and was a post-master's Fellow in Psychiatric Social Work at The Menninger Foundation in Topeka, Kansas. Following twenty years of direct clinical social work practice, he obtained a doctorate from Boston College Graduate School of Social Work and entered academic life. Currently he is an assistant professor at the Graduate School of Social Work and Social Research, Bryn Mawr College, where he teaches courses in life span development and clinical practice. Dr. Applegate is a member of the National Association of Social Workers, the Council on Social

Work Education, and the Pennsylvania Society for Clinical Social Work. He is a consulting editor for the *Child and Adolescent Social Work Journal*. His publications include several articles which reflect his interest in men's roles as caregivers across the life cycle.